# Other Books by Cathleen Rountree

*On Women Turning 70: Honoring the Voices of Wisdom*
*On Women Turning 60: Embracing the Age of Fulfillment*
*On Women Turning 50: Celebrating Midlife Discoveries*
*On Women Turning 40: Coming into Our Fullness*
*The Heart of Marriage: Discovering the Secrets of Enduring Love*
*50 Ways to Meet Your Lover: Following Cupid's Arrow*

# On Women Turning 30

# On Women Turning 30

## Making Choices, Finding Meaning

Interviews and Photography by
**Cathleen Rountree**

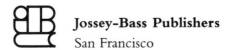
**Jossey-Bass Publishers**
San Francisco

OUACHITA TECHNICAL COLLEGE

Jossey-Bass books and products are available through most bookstores. To contact Jossey-Bass directly, call (888) 378-2537, fax to (800) 605-2665, or visit our website at www.josseybass.com.

Substantial discounts on bulk quantities of Jossey-Bass books are available to corporations, professional associations, and other organizations. For details and discount information, contact the special sales department at Jossey-Bass.

Manufactured in the United States of America.

Interior design by Paula Goldstein.

**Library of Congress Cataloging-in-Publication Data**

Rountree, Cathleen.
    On women turning 30 : making choices, finding meaning / Cathleen Rountree.— 1st ed.
        p. cm.
    ISBN 0-7879-5036-X (hc : acid-free paper)
    1. Women—United States—Psychology—Case studies. 2. Women—United States—Social conditions—Case studies. 3. Women—United States—Interviews. 4. Self-realization. 5. Adulthood. I. Title: On women turning thirty. II. Title.
    HQ1206 .R67 2000
    155.6'33—dc21                                                              99-050520

FIRST EDITION
*HB Printing*
10  9  8  7  6  5  4  3  2  1

# Contents

Introduction   1

Susana Herrera   9

Nell Newman   17

Susie Bright   31

Lisa Leeman   53

Francesca Ferrentelli   67

Monica Praba Pilar   85

Ikazo   97

Elisabeth Targ   107

Charlene Wolf   125

Terry Schneider   133

Kamala Deosaransingh   153

Katherine Spilde   163

Mima Lecocq   177

Randi Gray Kristensen   189

Kate Noonan   207

The Author   219

*For Leslie Berriman,*
*Best Editor and*
*Dear Friend*

# Acknowledgments

Having an editor who understands your work as a writer is a necessity (though one not always met); having an editor who truly appreciates your efforts is a rarity—and Leslie Berriman is such an editor. A thanks to Alan Rinzler, who inherited this project. I also wish to thank the various individuals and departments at Jossey-Bass Publishers who contributed their efforts to this book as well as to *On Women Turning 70,* especially Lasell Whipple, Kim Corbin, Amy Scott, Samya Sattar, Margaret Sebold, Jennifer Bendery, and Paula Goldstein.

My literary agent, Ellen Levine, is God's gift to the authors in her "stable." All writers should be so blessed to have someone like Ellen standing behind them, beside them, and in front of them when need be.

To my classmates at Pacifica Graduate Institute, I offer my warmest affection for your support, and I especially thank the cheerleading squad of Leah Friedman, Kwame Scruggs, Madeleine Waddell, Richard Stromer, Martha Peacock, Marie Elliot-Gartner, Francesca Ferrentelli, Karen St. Pierre, and Char Wolf.

My professors at Pacifica have been inspiring and encouraging. My sincere appreciation to Drs. Dennis Slattery, Kathleen Jenks, Ginette Paris,

Dawn George, Hendrika De Vries, Christine Downing, Patrick Mahaffey, Randi Gray Kristensen, Dan Noel, and David Miller. Also thanks to the numerous staff members on campus, especially Mark Kelly in the library; Sarah, Louise, and Bill in the bookstore; and Edie Barrett and Diane Huerta in administration.

I wish to offer my deepest gratitude to each woman who participated in *On Women Turning 30* and who gave so generously of her time, her wisdom, and her inspiring presence. I extend a very special thank you to Liz Smith, Mary Travers, and Riane Eisler for contributing their much appreciated endorsements for this book.

For services rendered in times of need, much appreciation to Mary Ann Soule, Hope Rhode, Dennis St. Peter, Doug Broyles (my computer god!), Alec Cast, Pat McAnaney, and Judy Rose of UCSC.

My friends continue to provide the love and nurturing that are my sustenance. My love and affection to Christiane Corbat, Deanne Burke, Michael Park and Kevin Connelley, Katherine Spilde, Lisa Leeman, Karen St. Pierre and Peter Samuels, Mary Ann Soule, Char Wolf, Maurine Doerken, Deena Metzger, Vicki Noble, Pat Zimmerman, Marie and Randy Kramer, and Manuel and Laura Gomes.

Lastly, my love and appreciation to the most incredible son a mother could have, Christian Wright, who just heals my heart. And to Sienna, my Mr. Wonderful.

In each of my books I have inevitably forgotten to mention someone hugely important to me in my life. Whoever you are, I thank you!

*Aptos, California*                                    CATHLEEN ROUNTREE
February 2000

# On Women Turning 30

# Introduction

What I found during the course of interviewing a variety of women in their thirties and writing this book is that the thirties is a highly performance–oriented, pressure-packed decade. It is not a decade of leisure. Women in their thirties are supposed to have put it all together: marriage, children, and, of course, a successful career. It is assumed that they launched their career in their twenties.

Susie Bright, the outspoken author of *The Sexual State of the Union* and her newest book on creating a personal sexual philosophy, *Full Exposure,* wondered, "When did this all happen? When did the thirties become such a pressure-filled time? It used to be that after thirty, women were getting their first divorce, already had kids, and were entering their forties with their kids grown up and leaving home. I think about how much things have changed in the past few decades. It seems as if everyone is supposed to be, or allowed to be, immature longer. Teenagers are treated like babies; twenty year olds are treated like teenagers; and yet when you reach your thirties, you're suddenly supposed to be superwoman. There are all these expectations. Women feel as if they have to squeeze in ambition between childhood and motherhood. It's relentless."

Who are women in their thirties? Unlike the decade of the forties and beyond, women in their thirties usually have not had the time necessary to make a name in their chosen field. Many of those who have, such as Camryn Manheim, Jodi Foster, Natasha Richardson, Alfre Woodard, Marisa Tomei, Mira Sorvino, Janet Jackson, Lili Taylor, Courtney Love, Emme, Calista Flockhart, Sarah McClaughlin, Jennifer Jason Leigh, Laura Dern, Bridget Fonda, Joan Chen, Emily Watson, Mariel Hemingway, Molly Ringwald, and Diva Cecilia Bartoli, are all in the arts and entertainment industry and have achieved celebrity status. Noted authors in their thirties are feminist spokeswoman Susan Faludi; Elizabeth Wurtzel, author of the best-selling *Prozac Nation* and *Bitch*; Helen Fielding, author of the best-selling novel about a thirty-something single woman, *Bridget Jones's Diary*; and Julia Alvarez, author of *In the Time of Butterflies*.

Other women are not yet well known but undoubtedly will be in the future, because they are pioneers pushing back frontiers of inquiry, technology, and gender. Chicago-based sexual harassment and discrimination attorneys Mary Stowell and Linda Friedman filed a class-action sex discrimination suit on behalf of twenty-three women against the brokerage house of Salomon Smith Barney, the second largest firm in the nation. The project manager, scientist, and engineer for the planetary exploration of Mars at the National Aeronautics and Space Administration, Sarah A. Gavit, Suzanne E. Smrekar, and Kari A. Lewis, are in their thirties or younger (Lewis is twenty-five). Margaret Edson wrote her play "Wit"—a story about the life and death of a John Donne scholar—when she was only thirty; it took her seven years to get it produced, but when she did, it was on Broadway and it received a Pulitzer Prize. Heather Mills was a British model until she lost her left leg in a pedestrian accident. She managed with extraordinary resilience to turn her misfortune into a powerful vehicle for helping others—one year later she founded the Heather Mills Health Trust to recycle artificial limbs to amputees from Croatia to Cambodia. Michelle Banks, a deaf African American actress, is the founder and Artistic Director of Onyx Theatre Company in Washington, D.C., the first deaf theatre company for People of Color in the United States. Michela Alioto, a charismatic young woman in her early thirties, has decided to follow in the footsteps of her high-profile political family to pursue a life in politics. This in itself is not unusual, but the fact that Michela has been wheelchair-bound since a ski-lift accident when she was seventeen left her paralyzed from the waist down is. Patricia Buttenheim and Ann Snoeyenbos, a nurse and reference librarian, respectively, from Manhattan, are ultra athletes who competed in the Double Ironman race (that's 4.8 miles of swimming, 224 miles of biking, and 52.4 miles of running—and these are consecutive events. The women's record, set in 1994, is 22 hours, 7 minutes.).

As mentioned earlier, some of the current trends for women in their thirties in the new millennium are that women in their thirties have postponed having children in their twenties. Of the fifteen women included here, twelve do not yet have children. Women are observing serial monogamy or marrying later than in past decades: of the fifteen women included here, thirteen are unmarried. Having come of age after the sexual revolution of the 1960s, women are experiencing more freedom in sexual orientation. Four of the women in this book consider themselves either lesbian or bisexual. If a desire for children precedes the actualization of a committed relationship or marriage, women are opting for single parenthood or, in the case of some lesbian mothers, opting for the choice of a two-mother family, rather than the traditional father-as-head-of nuclear family. One woman among the fifteen became pregnant as a single woman and made the choice to raise her child on her own; and another woman is helping to raise her female partner's child.

These are the women you will encounter and be inspired by in this book: Randi Gray Kristensen, an academic scholar; Susana Herrera and Kate Noonan, both teachers (Kate is also a performance artist and theater director and Susana is also a writer); Katherine Spilde, an anthropologist; Mima Lecocq, a chef and mother; Susie Bright, a writer and mother; Ikazo, a writer; Charlene Wolf, a mother and a student; Kamala Deosaransingh, a social activist; Lisa Leeman, a documentary filmmaker; Francesca Ferrentelli, a psychotherapist; Monica Praba Pilar, a visual and environmental artist; Nell Newman, Director of Newman's Own Organics and an environmental activist; Terry Schneider, a professional athlete and a trainer; and Elisabeth Targ, a psychiatrist.

Women who are in their thirties now are the first post–baby boom generation and the first generation to benefit fully from the second wave of the women's movement, which began with the publication of Betty Friedan's *The Feminine Mystique,* published in 1963. Using Naomi Wolf's, author of *The Beauty Myth,* definition of feminism—"Women's ability to think about their subjugated role in history, and then to do something about it"—all the women interviewed for this book have an awareness of what they owe to the feminist movement and consider themselves feminists.

There is a range of women in their thirties: those who are single and love it and are ensconced in a rewarding career and profession; those who are trying to do it all: marriage, children, and career; those who are married with three kids and have no professional life; those who are terrified that they will never marry and have children; those who choose to bear and raise or adopt children as single mothers; and women who have deliberately chosen a lesbian or bisexual lifestyle.

As always, class and geography still affect a woman's place in the world. "In Minnesota," according to Katherine Spilde, a participant in this book who was born and raised in Minnesota, "it may still be significant if a woman is unmarried by her thirties, whereas in California or New York City [both areas in which Katherine has also lived], the emphasis is not the same." In general, women in the middle class and above take for granted that they will attend college. If they do not, it is usually related to the class or economic system rather than to gender bias, as it was in the past.

There have been structural changes in terms of women's rights during the lifetime of these women: Title IX, which promotes equal funding for women in sports; the supposed shattering of the glass ceiling; and the Anita Hill–Clarence Thomas case, which brought attention to the issue of sexual harassment in the workforce. But it takes time for these new awarenesses to permeate society, so there is a lag in catching up to new freedoms. And although there may have been political emancipation, the backlash against women has taken a more subtle turn in symptoms, such as an increase in eating disorders. As the old structures fall, are women now taking the lead in holding themselves back by internalizing a patriarchal prejudice? Two of the women I interviewed for this book speak at length about eating disorders: Katherine Spilde of her own difficulties with anorexia, bulimia, and weight gain and loss and Francesca Ferrentelli of her experience as an eating disorders therapist. These have been the stereotypes about women in their thirties:

> The thirties is a decade of childbearing.
> If a woman isn't married yet, she's on her way to spinsterhood.
> Women should be settled in a career.
> The thirties is the time of "serious" (leading to marriage) dating.
> The biological time clock is ticking, and women feel a desperation
>     to have a traditional marriage before they can bring children into
>     the world.

What I have found about women in their thirties in the new millennium are that they postponed having children in their twenties; they may be exploring several careers before settling on one; in an era of AIDS and safer-sex consciousness, they are observing serial monogamy or marrying later than in past decades; having come of age after the sexual revolution of the 1960s, they are experiencing more freedom in sexual orientation; if a desire for children precedes the actualization of a committed relationship or marriage, women are opting for single parenthood or, in the case of some lesbian mothers, a two-mother family.

Most of the women in this book remain unmarried and childless: some by choice, some in the process of trying to conceive, some hoping for the magical remedy of the "right man" or relationship to answer their dilemma, some resigned, willingly or otherwise, to never having children. In contrast, I gave birth to my only child when I was twenty years old in 1969, went back to college in my mid-twenties, opened a restaurant at thirty, and went to graduate school in my late forties. By the time I was forty, my son was halfway through college. I had been married and divorced and had had three other long-term relationships.

I saw how tense many women in their late thirties are about "getting their life together." Some of those who are not in a relationship with a man feel a desperation as their biological clock ticks away—"like a New York taxi meter," Francesca Ferrentelli put it. Curiously, it used to be the forties, a time when women's looks begin to change noticeably, that this desperation set in. Now the big questions for women in their thirties are these: Why aren't you married? Why aren't you fit? Why aren't you pregnant? Why aren't you producing (kids, work, career)?

Many women are taking this question of children to a new level. Examples of well-known women who have chosen to have children on their own as single mothers are Jodi Foster, Diane Keaton, Sinead O'Connor, Linn Ullman (daughter of Liv Ullman and Ingmar Bergman), and of course the most public of all single mothers, Madonna, who contributed to the debate on family values that both major American political parties have addressed.

One of the major changes to have marked the second half of the twentieth century has probably been the erosion, for better or worse, of the nuclear family unit. In 1950, only 4 percent of American babies were born to mothers who were not married, and the stigma of birth out of wedlock was so great that many of them were placed for adoption. Now, according to Melissa Ludtke, in her book, *On Our Own: Unmarried Motherhood in America,* almost a third of births—more than a million children a year—are to unmarried women, a change that has sparked bitter national debate over everything from sex roles to welfare reform. As a means for art to answer this question, in the 1999 novel by Elizabeth Berg, *Talk Before Sleep,* the thirty-six-year-old protagonist is Patty Anne Murphy, a real estate agent who is single and wants a baby more than anything else. Her solution? Convince her gay best friend, Ethan Allen Gaines, who has also struck out trying to find a partner, to give parenthood a shot together. They do.

Recently a friend sent me a quotation from a newspaper about Lifetime television and its new executives. It quoted Gloria Steinem as saying: "Lifetime is very valuable. It celebrates women's power. For their profiles, viewers would be quite interested in women who are not famous. There should be more profiles on interesting, worthwhile women who are not famous."

Most of the women I have chosen to include in this book are interesting, worthwhile women who are not famous. All of them are interesting because they are passionately living their lives, fully engaged. No matter what your age as the reader, each woman will inspire you with her energy, enthusiasm, and commitment. The women in this book, each in her own way, are making choices and finding meaning.

Turning thirty for me was the opportunity for a new start. I felt this was going to be my decade: Carpe diem—seize the day. Finally, a new opportunity to experience a different way of expressing myself. It's a marking place, a turning point, a way to begin over.

SUSANA HERRERA

# Susana Herrera

## PROFILE

"*Jam bah doo nah*?" Susana Herrera asks me whenever we talk on the phone or when she e-mails me. "Are you in your skin?" or "Is your soul in your body?" is the greeting she learned from the friends she made among the Tapouri people of northern Cameroon during the two years she was a Peace Corps volunteer in a West African village. Susana's infectious good spirits make her the personification of the terms *ebullient* ("boiling up") and *enthusiastic* ("possessed by God"). Whether she is talking about her writing, teaching, fiancé, or long-distance running, Susana's thirty-year-old vigor and passion inspire those lucky enough to be around her.

In *Mango Elephants in the Sun: How Life in an African Village Let Me Be in My Skin,* Susana (or Suzannedee, as her French-speaking Cameroon friends and I call her) writes about living in West Africa and also incorporates her childhood upbringing and her personal spiritual quest for enlightenment. She calls her West African self "a machete-swingin', snake-killin', termite-eatin' woman." After fully growing "into her skin" during this two-year adventure, Susana, who lives in Santa Cruz, wondered who she would be when she returned "home."

**9**

Who she became is a writer of surreal experiences in distinctive prose. With *Mango Elephants in the Sun,* published the month she turned thirty, she has definitely tapped into some mango magic. At the world's largest book fair, in Frankfurt, Germany, all several hundred copies of her book were eagerly gathered up, and the publisher, Shambhala, has already sold the foreign rights to translations in Chinese and Taiwanese. It's impossible to believe that another dozen or so countries won't also wish to buy the rights soon. And then, of course, there is the screenplay that Susana has written from the novel, which she has sent to two Hollywood producers and to the actress Jennifer Lopez, whom she would like to see in the starring role as (who else?) Susana Herrera.

Our living close has allowed Susana and me to become friends and writing partners. As she works on her second novel, *Laughing Girl, Howling Woman,* a story about her parents' lives and her childhood, I too am writing my own novel about my childhood, *Every Soul Is a Circus.* We share a love of adventure, music, movies, food, exercise, and, of course, writing.

In her interview, Susana speaks eloquently and openly about her writing, her love for her fiancé, John David Guillory, her teaching, her spiritual life, and finding meaning in a difficult past, all with a highly developed sense of humor.

## Adventure with Meaning

I was born in St. Albans, New York, on May 15, 1969. My father was Irish and French, and my mother is Navajo and Spanish. I lived in New Orleans, Louisiana, until I was seven years old and spent my adolescence in Fremont, in the Bay Area. Finally, at fifteen, I found my home in Santa Cruz, California, and here is where my heart is.

I survived being raped as a seven-year-old child, sexually abused for three years by a stepfather, and emotionally and physically abused by a father who was mentally unstable, severely depressed, and suicidal. My father eventually killed himself on my sixteenth birthday in the city I was born in. I lived through an abusive marriage until finally I mustered up the strength to leave and get a divorce.

These challenges that I have overcome in my life have made me stronger and have carved depth into my soul. That is where the writer was born and emerged from the inner chambers of my heart. I had to find something to hold on to while I went through each event in my life. Writing and reading saved my soul. It was what kept me alive, kept me going, kept something from within me from being snuffed out.

As a child, I read to remind myself that I was alive but to forget my life. I read to know that there were opportunities for another way of choosing to live my life. I read to find out about love and to experience it from some-where—anywhere. I read to discover the heroines so that I could know that I too could be a hero. Toni Morrison with her words from *Beloved*—"Be your own best thing"—and Maya Angelou's *I Know Why the Caged Bird Sings* let me know that other young girls have been raped and have lived to tell about it. The writings of Alice Walker, Zora Neale Hurston, Sandra Cisneros, Chinua Achebe, and Gloria Anzaldua have also had great influence on my writing.

After graduating from the University of California at Santa Cruz in 1992, I went into the Peace Corps and was sent to Cameroon in West Africa. My Peace Corps experience has been the greatest personal experience in my life. It made me bloom in a way I'd never before stretched. I became the woman I always believed that I was. I became my soul and got the closest look at my own true nature. It was there that I found myself again—as if I'd been lost for a very long time. It was as if I had awakened from a deep sleep and slowly stood back up and began the long process of transformation—like going into the cocoon to become the butterfly. It was in the desert of a remote vil-lage that I learned to breathe, learned to heal, and learned to get over the ghosts haunting my dreams.

*Mango Elephants in the Sun* was the culmination of my childhood up-bringing and my own personal spiritual quest for enlightenment. In Africa, everything that I learned looked me straight in the eyes. I learned what it meant to be in the moment and to be in my skin.

I was born into a family of spiritual seekers. My mother left home at age eleven to be a Catholic nun and spent the next ten years in the convent. When he was only seven years old, my father decided to be a Trappist monk; later he became a Carthusian monk and then finally a Catholic priest. My mother and father met in their early twenties in nursing school, and both decided to leave their vocations before making their final vows in order to be married. Later my father turned to Zen Buddhism and moved our family into the Zen Center of Los Angeles. It was here that I learned to sit Zazen [in silent meditation], meditate on a koan [a Buddhist parable], pursue a spiritual practice, and just be. I grew up greatly by the life and words of Jesus and the teaching of Buddha.

I love the Father Mother God with all my heart. I love being alive. I love my fiancé. I love making love to my fiancé. I love Ben and Jerry's Real Ice Cream. I love writing. I love running. I love my family and friends. I love being alone and quiet. I love opera, especially *Madame Butterfly*. I love classical music and jazz. I love the film *Harold and Maude*.

My greatest happiness has been falling in love with my fiancé, John David Guillory, and with life itself. My deepest sorrow has been my father's suicide. The wound of the heart goes deeper than any physical wound.

My advice to other women with visions and passions who want to pursue them is to go be by yourself for awhile. Leave the country. Have an adventure. Heal from the pain. Get over it. Move on. Forgive. Bless them. Embrace yourself. Fall in love with your soul. Talk to God. Pray. Listen to God. Pray some more. Express your creativity. Go deeper. Go deeper still. Laugh a lot. Cry about the world. Don't let anything stop you from expressing your wild soul and crazy heart.

My lifestyle right now is about work, work, and work. I work a lot. I teach high school full time, and I run and I write in the evenings. I correct papers and write on the weekends. I am trying to sleep more and be on the phone less. I try to see the ocean every day and say hello to a tree. My daily routine is to run first thing in the morning, teach all day, and write in the evenings and squeeze in as much reading and movie watching that I can with spoonfuls of ice cream and handfuls of popcorn. With all that, I try to stay in touch with friends and family as much as I can, but I seem to fall short often. I have been blessed with juicy and succulent people in my life and feel that I don't have enough time to do everything that my heart is telling me to do. I miss a lot of holidays and events, but that is what I have to do right now in my life when I work two full-time jobs.

When I get older, I want to be like Maude (the Ruth Gordon character in *Harold and Maude*). I want to be sexy. I want to make love often. I want to take risks and celebrate life. I want to be less afraid of making a fool out of myself, looking silly, making mistakes. I want to be able to sing out loud in front of people and dance with grace and without a care. I am deadly afraid of both of those.

I want to get to a point where I help to make others successful. I want to aid others in finding their own inner light and authentic self and to live their dreams from that place.

On my thirtieth birthday, my first book was published, and I did my first book signing while celebrating my engagement to John with my family and friends—truly, the happiest I have ever been in my life. I last surprised myself by being speechless and moved to tears by the "I love you, Suzi" from my stepson, Jordan Guillory. The tenderness of my love for this child who is not my blood amazes me. I can't say that I know a parent's love for his or her own child, but this certainly comes close.

And I just finished writing a screenplay—something that I've wanted to do since I was in the fourth grade. I want to travel around the world for two years. I want to master Spanish, and I want to get a Ph.D. in literature and teach at a university.

Turning thirty for me was the opportunity for a new start. I felt this was going to be my decade: Carpe diem—seize the day. Finally, a new opportunity to experience a different way of expressing myself. It's a marking place, a turning point, a way to begin over. It's different from earlier decades because I've experienced more, learned from it. I'm not being unrealistic in my expectations of myself and love. The goals that I have for my thirties are based on soul growth and being on the journey and loving every minute of it. I think previous decades are about satisfying our thirst to experience all of what we are. I am more selective in my experiences now. I no longer want just thrills; I'm looking for adventure with meaning. I no longer look in someone else's eyes for the love I need; instead, I embrace myself. I no longer achieve goals to prove something to myself of who I am and what I am capable of. I no longer identify myself as first and foremost a physical being. I understand that the seat of my being is in my soul. I am spirit first. I am not a human body with a soul inside it but a soul having a human experience.

The women I know are healing; they are doing the work. They are not looking to others for answers or predictions of their future successes. They are turning within and finding the answers inside, trusting their own voice more than someone else's. They are realizing their power and making their light shine. They are making peace with their pasts and living from a sense that they know that the future is full of light and joy and its being taken care of and they are trusting their own intuition and dreams more and more.

The second wave of the women's movement made it possible for me to identify with my heritage and explore my history. I changed my name from Suzanne Smith to Susana Herrera for my writer's name, taking my mother's maiden name and being proud to wear it.

My relationship with my body is better than it's ever been. It seemed that as soon as I really began to love me for me and forgive myself and heal, the extra weight I was carrying just dropped off. I began to look and walk like my real self, and I believe that loving my body made me a lighter person. That's when it began to feel really good to be in my skin.

John and I want to have two children, but I have so much to do in my thirties that I think children will be in my forties. I simply don't have time right now even to think about the idea. Having Jordan in my life is a joy and gives me the opportunity to live from that playful child heart space when he's with us.

My spiritual practice is a mixture of this and that. I do regular meditation; I run; I write in my journal every day. I am doing what I came here to do as a teacher and a writer. I do muscle balance exercises and work with a trainer. I am a part of Inner Light Ministries. I work very closely with a woman in healing, hypnotherapy, and listening to the inner voice and creativity.

In the next decade, I look forward to writing three more novels and four screenplays. I'd like to see Ben and Jerry come out with a Mango Elephants in the Sun Ice Cream. I'd like to see my screenplay made into a film starring Jennifer Lopez and Djimon Housou, the wonderful actor from *Amistad*. I'd like to travel around the world with my partner.

I look forward to feeling at peace in the mist of chaos, understanding that it's just PMS that's making me feel this way, and being OK with doing nothing all day and being able to think of funny, witty lines at the exact right time. I look forward to understanding more and more that I am a human in progress, giving myself more permission to take risks and be more vulnerable.

I also look forward to becoming a better cook, having less guilt, spending more time having fun and less time working. And I look forward to someday being able to say to myself, "You are enough," and really mean it.

*I felt compelled to do something contributive when I started this business, and I still do. But the product came out of my being such a pessimist about the state of the world and being very depressed about it in my teens and twenties, to the point where the only outlet for me was to do something to make a difference. Otherwise I couldn't exist.*

NELL NEWMAN

# Nell Newman

## PROFILE

When she isn't working at her desk in the Santa Cruz office of Newman's Own Organics, the company she runs with partner Peter Meehan, Nell Newman might be found surfing at Paradise Cove or flying a friend's falcon or shopping for produce at the local farmers' market or deep-sea fishing for salmon and tuna or, as in this case, doing an interview to promote the cause of organic agriculture.

Organic means that no pesticides and no artificial fertilizers have been used on a crop for at least three years, and the food continues pesticide free all the way through processing. Nell is so committed to the organic method of food production that she has a paper trail for all her products, from farmer to shelf. You may have seen (and, if you are lucky, sampled) some of the six-year-old company's products: Fig Newmans, Pretzels, Champion Chip Cookies, a variety of organic chocolate bars, and, my personal favorite, Jalapeño Tortilla Chips.

The first time I saw Nell was in 1968, when she was nine years old and acting in *Rachel, Rachel,* a film directed by her father, Paul Newman, and starring her mother, Joanne Woodward. The second time I saw her was in 1972, in *The Effect of Gamma Rays on Man-in-the-Moon Marigolds* (same director, same actress), a film so true to my own damaged mother-daughter relationship that I have never forgotten it. The third time was when we met at Kelly's, a local bakery, to discuss her current work.

When I asked what had happened to her promising acting career, Nell was quick to say, "I was more interested in animals and nature than movies." Especially the peregrine falcon. And, indeed, it was her love for falcons and other bird life that propelled her to launch Newman's Own Organics. "When you see whole populations of birds like falcons and eagles reduced, and even endangered, by pesticides, you have to believe there's a less harmful way to grow food," she said.

Many years after her father's successful company, Newman's Own, was established, Nell approached her father with the idea for an organics division. He was skeptical about the importance of and difference in organic foods, but Nell convinced him and the rest of her family with an all-organic Thanksgiving feast. Newman's Own Organics was on its way. Newman's Own distributes its after-tax profits to charitable organizations around the world—$90 million so far—and so does Newman's Own Organics. Nell donates to her own favorite charities: the Organic Farming Research Foundation, the Predatory Bird Research Group, the Renewable Resources Institute (which helps towns, cities, and states do green plans), and, among others, the Surfer's Environmental Alliance.

By the end of our time together outside Kelly's, it was clear that Nell's focus had shifted. With her nine-and-a-half-foot "long board" stuffed in her Subaru station wagon, she was ready to hit the surf.

## Making a Difference

Newman's Own Organics basically came out of a tremendous need. I came in at the tail end of a project that was reestablishing the peregrine falcon. The group had been collecting eggs, hatching them, and releasing the birds for fifteen years. They had put over eight hundred birds out into the wild and established 120 pairs, and now the project was going into the monitoring stage. Although the birds out there now are successful at hatching their young and the population has been increasing, the environment still has residual DDT, and we still don't know the implications of all the other pesticides we're putting out. But we couldn't get grant proposals to monitor. It drove me crazy. Why did they think the birds went extinct in the first place? Because nobody's keeping an eye on them. It's crucial to maintaining the integrity of the population and determining whether or not there were actually any effects going on. If you weren't actually spending any money to monitor very closely, you wouldn't know.

The response I got all the time as I was trying to fundraise was, "Well, you've already established them." So I thought, "I'm sick and tired of trying to raise money; I want to be able to give it away." There was a certain amount of frustration and a need for funding, for monitoring, specifically for biological research. It's not necessarily the fault of foundations that they don't have enough of the bio background to understand implications, or maybe it was my fault for not being clear enough. It could be a wide variety of things. They could have just thought they'd funded it for five years and didn't want to fund it anymore, but I had a really hard time seeing all this effort going into it and then not being able to get continued support. That was part of it.

The other part was that we were putting birds back out into an environment which still had residual DDT, and now that bad egg shell thinning was on the decline, the birds that are out there are successful at hatching their young—there had not been a lot of money spent for egg shell testing, etc. But the population has been increasing. We still don't know the implications of all the other pesticides we're putting out.

So this need for organic came into my mind. Maybe I could start a business, donate the profit to charity, and support the growth of organic agriculture, which would help not just bird of prey populations but many different species, including humans. The birds of prey are always portrayed as the canaries in the coal mine.

Now we have biotech to screw things up, too. That's sort of taken all the fun out of the industry for me in the past couple of months. In my youth I had a really naive picture of what I was doing, but I had a lot of energy and commitment to it. As a fundraiser and a falconer, it was something I had an innate connection to.

The hardest thing about my work has been that I spent my life avoiding the public eye and now I'm wallowing in it. It's probably trivial in view of the bigger picture, but personally it's been hard—just having to deal with it for so long and avoiding it for most of my life and then sort of opening up the big door to wallow in it. I have to remind myself a lot that I have a purpose. I've gotten used to that. That's the downside.

Surfing and falconry offer the same refuge. I don't get this odd, fearful knot in the pit of my stomach anymore unless the surf is wild. I used to get it when I was flying my bird, because every time you fly your bird, you risk losing it. It puts you out in nature; you can't think of anything else. It put me in touch with the natural realm that I enjoyed so much, and now that I don't have a bird, surfing has really done that. I rarely think of work when I'm floating around on my surfboard. Just me and that great expanse of sky and the incoming waves.

I always tell people, "The ocean doesn't give a shit whose daughter I am." It's going to try and kill you no matter what. It doesn't make judgments about who your parents are. For me there's something really refreshing about that. Every time I get held under and almost drown in the ocean and tumble, I'm reminded that we are actually all equal. That's why I love it.

I'm definitely my father's daughter because I went to race car driving school, but he wouldn't let me race. I went when I was twenty-three. Three days of road in Atlanta, and on the third day there was a guy who was watching who had a car that he was going to run at mid-Ohio, which is a twenty-four-hour race with three drivers. He came up to me, said, "You know you're really good; would you like to be my third driver for the twenty-four hours mid-Ohio." I was like, "Yes, I got a ride. Dad guess what? I got a ride." He's like, "Get back to college; you can't do that." He let me take the training because it's great for learning to drive on the road. Being a defensive driver, knowing how to stop, knowing what to do in a spin, how to catch a car—all those things you never learn in driver's ed are really crucial for surviving the road. Having rolled so many cars in my youth, it was probably a good thing.

Growing up, I went back and forth to school on either coast every other year. They were always good schools, but I missed algebra and diagramming sentences. Either I snowed teachers, which I couldn't possibly have done when I was very young, or they just let me slide. By the time I was a sophomore, I was so far behind in so many different areas that I was too frustrated and I didn't want to go back to school. I went to live in New York and then went and did a peregrine falcon release site and finally went back to college in my twenties.

I got a degree in human ecology from College of the Atlantic in Bar Harbor, Maine. Basically, it was exactly what I'd been looking for: taking the knowledge learned in college—in whatever area—and taking into account man's impact on the environment within the scope of whatever those studies are—as an architect, say, or an environmentalist. It was basically a biology degree for me, but a little bit broader.

I had a wonderful, crazy biology teacher named Butch Ramal, who would intimidate his students. He had this huge pile of books and would say, "This is the course load for the class," and he'd drop them on the floor and then walk out. That would be it. That would always scare off any riff-raff. People who knew better, because he had a reputation of being an incredible teacher, would still take his courses. His office hours were between 5:30 and 8:30 A.M. at the local diner. If you took his class, you met with him once or twice a week at the diner in your designated slot of time in which you would sit down and discuss a project or brainstorm and end up with all these place mats that had scribbles on them from Butch going on with these ideas and fluid dynamics on the place mat. He gave 110 percent and expected the same in return.

When I graduated from college, I worked for three months at the Environmental Defense Fund in New York and put together a recycling database. I loved the people I was working with, but when New York had its first big heat wave in a long time, I said, "I'm outta here." Living in New

York was hard enough; living in New York during a heat wave was miserable. My boyfriend, James, and I had gone to San Francisco a lot and loved it there, so we thought, "Why don't we just drive cross country?" So we left and drove across the country.

I was going to apply for a position with the Environmental Defense Fund in Oakland that was basically dealing with water rights issues. But I barely grasped the difficulty of the situation, and although it was a wonderful group of people there, they were real hotshots and I found them intimidating. So I called my friend Brian Walton, who sat on the board of the Peregrine Fund with me, and was talking to him about my trying to figure out what to do with my life, and he said, "There's a job opening up down here in Big Sur running the Ventana Wilderness Sanctuary." Brian did the first interview, and then I was interviewed the second time by the board of directors, and they were gung-ho. "She can get money from Newman's Own so that's a good thing." I had never done any fundraising, but I had a biology background and was a falconer. It was one of those odd things where people take you based on maybe false pretense, but it worked out. I did a kind of out-of-body experience—they voted, said, "Yes, we'd love to have you," and they were talking about my responsibilities: do all the fundraising, balance the budget, publish the quarterly newsletter. I worked there for two years. Then I moved on to fundraise for the predatory bird research group and did that for about two years too.

As the fundraising began to get more and more difficult, I started to figure out what to do. I started Newman's Own Organics when I was thirty-three with Peter, my business partner. He jokingly refers to himself as the man behind the curtain. I'm the one who gets to do all the interviews. Pete's the guy who does all the marketing and distribution, which is all the real grunt work.

Now, with all this biotech going—75,000,000 acres of bioengineered crops are being grown in the U.S. right now by Monsanto and Navarez—I feel less confident. Monsanto bioengineered a soybean to withstand higher doses of the herbicide Round-up so you have this soybean you can spray twice as much of an herbicide on. Now there are cross-pollination problems between conventional and organic soybeans. [As a result,] they're looking at buffer zones between 660 feet to 5 miles, as if the wind's going to stop blowing after 5 miles. It's become a real difficult question.

I would love Newman's Own Organics to get as big as Newman's Own. We've been at it for seven years, but our market is only one-tenth of what conventional grocery is. It's probably an unrealistic goal, but certainly something I strive for anyway. I think our products have tremendous potential. It would have more potential if we weren't having this constraint with biotech right now.

I felt compelled to do something contributive when I started this business, and I still do. But in fact the product came out of my being such a pessimist about the state of the world and being very depressed about it in my teens and twenties, to the point where the only outlet for me was to do something to make a difference. Otherwise I couldn't exist. Finally, I thought I couldn't exist anymore without making my contribution in some way, shape, or form. That contribution can be relative, I think, in so many different ways. It's just a matter of being good at something or happy. Being really good at something that makes you happy. It doesn't have to be anything that contributes if you don't want it to be. I certainly understand that concept too. I happen to come from a family where that drive is fairly strong, but it isn't for everybody.

To me, spiritual satisfaction is the most important thing. If you're content with yourself, then what else do you need? Ten years of sitting in meditation has been really good for me. It's given me a very different perspective about my neuroses, living the past, present, and future all at the same time, and it's given me a tremendous amount of focus when I do Zen sitting consistently, which I don't do often. I always end up saying, "I need to sit more." I need to put my sitting bench somewhere where I'll remember to sit on it and meditate on it rather than just use it for sitting on to watch TV or do my bills. I need more of a sacred spot.

I'd like to encourage people to eat organic. People always say, "God, it's so expensive; I can't afford it." It's actually much closer to the true cost of food because organic farmers don't get farm subsidies. When you reach for that loaf of white bread on the shelf of the supermarket, you think 79 cents is a great deal, but what you forget is that you already paid for that in the form of farm subsidies with your tax dollars. Your tax dollars just made that loaf of bread 79 cents as opposed to $1.29 or $1.59.

Organic is more expensive because it's labor intensive. Things have to be weeded. And that stuff weeded by hand maintains a clean environment and provides a livelihood for more people as opposed to corporate farming. It creates much less environmental degradation and such a strong economy for local farms and for local economies to maintain the food source within that area. The environment is in a natural stasis, as opposed to those who are constantly amending with nitrogen, no humus added back to the soil. It's not a natural state, and it's not sustainable in the long run. That's what's important. The naysayers will say, "The planet is growing so quickly; you can't feed the planet using organic agriculture. You won't be able to do it." Well, you can't even make that comparison until you have equal funding over equal time. The USDA [United States Department of Agriculture] has funded billions of dollars in conventional agricultural research over the past fifty years. Billions. When the Organic Farming Research Foundation did its study of USDA funding that would meet the criteria of organic, it was one-tenth of 1 percent of the 1993 budget. That information is not readily available to the public. Until there's equal funding over equal time, you can never actually make the comparison.

The Rodale Institute did a ten-year study looking at organic versus conventional farming and discovered over time that there were equal yields except during times of drought, when the organic farm produced higher yields because it had soil that held moisture. Whereas if you're just putting in granular nitrogen and you've got no worms—nothing living in your conventional soil—guess what? It can't tolerate drought. Some of that stuff is such a no-brainer, but there are some big naysayers who are very vocal about better living through plastics and pesticides. A guy with the Hudson Institute put out a book, *Better Living Through Plastics and Pesticides.* That's actually the title of a book. They're very vocal about it.

The rural economy of the United States is under strong attack from corporate farming. You've probably been through those little ghost towns where there's not anything left there but a big Wal-Mart on the edge of town and there's nothing left downtown. They're destroying our rural fabric, and that's where your food comes from. If we don't continue to support our rural fabric as much as possible, what are we going to end up with?

One of the organizations we're going to fund is a farmer who's a psychologist and lives in Iowa. He was discussing the number of farmers who commit suicide. People are killing themselves because they can't handle the stress of losing their farms.

There's got to be a better way. I don't think corporate pig farms are the better way. It's a very David and Goliath issue. I believe in supporting local and organic farmers as much as possible. It's a tough one for me because I'm very committed to organic agriculture, but there are a lot of small farmers who aren't. I say to them, "Are you thinking about doing this?" and discussing organics with them, helping them consider it is a good thing.

At the local farmers' market, I buy oranges, pomegranates, and peaches from a really old guy who drives up from Fresno. He's not organic. This man's worked so hard all his life, and I feel as if I need to support him. So as much as I am an organic convert, the local farm economy requires a tremendous amount of support too.

I didn't really like my acting career as a child. It never intrigued me the way natural history did. I did go to acting school for about a year and two months. My mom made me go to the neighborhood playhouse where she went to school, and I was terrified the whole time. I did two movies: *Rachel, Rachel* and *The Effect of Gamma Rays on Man-in-the-Moon Marigolds.* I'd grown up on movie sets, of course. It was not difficult for me; there's something about being on the set and acting on a working set. I was so familiar with it, even at age thirteen, that it was never a stretch.

I was never intimidated by the camera. Dad was an incredible director. Working with my mother was unbelievable. It was very easy. Then to go to acting school where you're sitting in a classroom with thirty or forty other people doing scenes was terrifying—I hated it. You'd have a teacher who'd say, "Stop. You did that wrong. You didn't have the right intent." But the right intent—you don't even have to find the right intent when you're thirteen years old and you're on the set with your family. I never could make that transition. I think people build up so many layers of protective mechanisms between the ages of eight and twenty, and I was not willing to let any of them down. I was frightened and didn't really want to do it. Even though they invited me back the next year, I was in acting school for only two months. One of the professors said something nasty to me, and I left. It wasn't that important to me, much to my parents' dismay, although they didn't say it at the time. Now both of them have.

The other intimidating thing was watching Mom in *Three Faces of Eve* while I was in acting school. "Forget it," I said. "I will never, ever be able to do that." I would watch her in that stunning, incredible performance. That whole scene where she comes in as the little prim, proper wife; then she cries, and she puts her head down like this, and when she looks up she's the other woman. The transformation is so profound that her whole face, her body language changes. Puts her legs up and removes her stockings. Oh, my God, I'll never be able to do that. She scared me off. That was a reality check, one way or the other.

But acting just didn't intrigue me. I had a really good time when I was doing the other pieces. But it did point out to me that what I really wanted to do was something in the realm of biology, not in acting. It narrowed my direction.


My position on children is that the world's an overpopulated place, and that's always been my theory—that there are too many people on the planet anyway. Of course, hitting forty now, it's been harder to deal with, and I have not come to a clear decision on it. I have two nephews whom I adore. My sister sent me a photograph on the outside of a package last year on my birthday present, so I put it in my wallet. If I don't have children, I'm going to be a wonderful aunt. I *am* a wonderful aunt. Unfortunately, they live back East. When my sister, Lissy, had her first baby, she had Mom; our Aunt Mary Jane—who isn't really our aunt but everybody from the South is an aunt; our maid, Carolyn, who's my mom's age and has been with us since we were really little, who thought she'd had her first grandchild; Carolyn's replacement,

Jenny, who raised eight children of her own; and Lissy's husband, Raf, who's a school teacher and loves to change diapers. She had four strong-willed women, four strong, very successful women, and Raf. That was her extended family. And my dad. That makes it appear very easy. I don't have that out here.

I do miss my family terribly, but I can't stand Westport [Connecticut] anymore, where I grew up. It's not my lifestyle. I could fish there; they do great fly-fishing in Long Island Sound but no surfing. I told my dad last time, "You know, if there were only waves on Long Island Sound and I could have a life-death experience in the ocean on a daily basis, I could probably stand Westport." I love Santa Cruz; I would have a really hard time moving. I surf or go for a paddle almost every day. My parents always say, "You can go surfing on Nantucket or someplace on the tip of Long Island." I miss them heartily, but I'm just torn—and running a business here.

My therapist says, "Thirty-nine is the crack between two worlds" and that it's really good to get to the other side of forty. Thirties were good, but I was really happy to get to forty—a lot of contentment. Thirties were a time of turmoil for me—turmoil in terms of both my personal and business lives. There was hard work and the ending of a ten-year relationship. In a lot of ways, it was very positive, but it was a lot of turmoil. That's why I took up meditating, Vapassana [a form of Buddhist meditation]. I've done maybe ten retreats—two ten-days and a bunch of shorter ones. I haven't done one since the ten-day one at Christmas when I was home. Surfing is a very meditative form. It's centering and calming—unless you're getting drowned.

That happened to me this summer. I'd been getting very cocky and catching a lot of big waves, a little bit overhead, but I had more cockiness than ability. I don't remember if I was trying to dive under a wave or if I wiped out on a wave, but I held my breath and was being rolled around—not somersaulted but up and down, rolled around a couple of feet underneath a very large wave. I was trying to be relaxed and could feel myself coming back up, and it was a really good thing because my lungs were about to pop. Then right when I came up, the back end of the wave pushed me back down again. It got dark, because I was far enough down. You can sense the light to darkness, and I was really scared. I got back up when my lungs were about to pop; it felt as if it took me a *really* long time to get my breath back. I think I was actually trying to dive under a really big wall of foam with my long board, which is a hard thing to do. It was very humbling. I just went and paddled off to the side, sat on the outside, and tried to catch my breath and made myself go back out and catch another wave before I went back in. But it definitely humbled me and made me chicken for a fair amount of time. Luckily I went to Cabo San Lucas in Baja, California, afterward and surfed in warm water.

About aging, I have this remarkable role model already in my life. And I've been blessed with good genes. My parents are both very healthy and fit. It's not something I worry about. I've gotten to forty in one piece except for a bike accident, which left me with crow's feet on this side and none on this side because I bruised all the skin off the left side of my face; I keep thinking, "Do I need a face peel on the other side because I already got a face peel on this side?" Having made it through the bicycle accident, which happened when I was thirty and feeling very fit from surfing, I've been very lucky. I've been blessed. I have a very dear business partner who works his butt off and unfortunately is a workaholic; I can never work as hard as he can, but I think the types of work we do are very different. Mine is much more personal in nature, but I'm so blessed to have Pete because he is such a godsend in terms of doing the nitty-gritty stuff that I couldn't do. I couldn't balance the books. Pete likes doing things like that. He handles all those things that I can't handle doing. I live in a beautiful place, and I have a wonderful family I see often. I just feel blessed. I don't have any concerns about aging at this point in my life. I am actually very content with myself at this point, so I consider myself lucky.

"Do whatever makes you happy" is a good definition of success. My siblings all do very different things. My sister, Lissy, is an absolutely brilliant artist who I don't think has ever sold a single piece of her work. She does everything from clay to painting. The best stuff she has is still in our family. Now she is producing all the grandchildren and is an incredible mom. In my eyes, she is incredibly successful, but in a totally different realm from what I'm doing. Success is what you make it. I think I would be very happy fishing and surfing and having a big garden and flying a falcon. I could be very happy and consider myself very successful doing that—which I probably will do at some point in my life.

*When you're in your thirties, you've been around the block; you've learned something. You've loved; you've hated. You've probably had your heart broken. You are tempered a little bit by some harsh experiences, but you still have such a reserve of strength. I used to think, because of that thing about not trusting anybody over thirty, that there was a sense of being such an old fogy. Thirty is not fogy; thirty is still kicking around in the buttercups if you want to. I didn't enter my thirties knowing who I was going to be or having the reputation for anything. At the end of it, I did.*

SUSIE BRIGHT

# Susie Bright

## PROFILE

Susie Bright claims that her first publication was in 1967, when she wrote a passionate pamphlet against Ronald Reagan with her orange-red Crayola and distributed it up and down her neighborhood block. Her family moved back and forth between the San Francisco Bay Area and Los Angeles, with a teenage hiatus to Edmonton, Alberta.

In 1975, when she was seventeen, she dropped out of high school in Los Angeles and started traveling around the country working as a radical community organizer and trade union activist.

At Cal State Long Beach, she studied theater and women's studies and graduated from the University of California at Santa Cruz with a B.A. in community studies in 1981. She moved to San Francisco and lived there for the next fifteen years, where she joined what she calls a "lefty queer political group" called Stonewall and a coalition of queer artists called Mainstream Exiles, both of which produced some memorable and controversial events in the early 1980s.

In 1981, she got a part-time retail clerk job at Good Vibrations, the famous feminist sex toy emporium, where she also pursued training as a sex educator. In 1983, she was contacted by two women, Debi Sundahl and Myrna Elana, who were creating a new magazine "for the adventurous lesbian," called *On Our Backs.* After the first issue in 1984, she became the chief editor of the magazine and devoted herself to the small company until April 1991. While still at *On Our Backs,* she created two show-and-tell film performances, one about lesbian erotica, *All Girl Action,* and another called *How to Read a Dirty Movie,* both in collaboration with her then-partner, the photographer-filmmaker Honey Lee Cottrell.

In 1986, she was offered a job at one of *Penthouse*'s small magazines, *Forum,* to write reviews of porn movies. She became the first mainstream female, not to mention feminist, porn critic. She began her first book with Joani Blank, the owner of Good Vibrations, who also operated Down There Press. *Herotica* was a collection of contemporary women-authored erotic fiction, an entirely new idea at the time. A new genre was born, and Susie continued the Herotica series, editing two more editions released by Plume/Penguin.

In 1990, Cleis Press, a small lesbian publisher, asked if she would like to put together a collection of her popular "Susie Sexpert" sex advice and columns that she had been writing for *On Our Backs* over the years. *Susie Sexpert's Lesbian Sex World,* the first book of her own writing, became a best-seller and somewhat of a "manual for a generation of dykes."

In 1995, she accepted an appointment to teach a course in The Politics of Sexual Representation at the University of California at Santa Cruz. She enjoyed Santa Cruz so much that she moved there with her daughter and partner, Jon Bailiff. Her other books have been *Susie Bright's Sexual Reality*; *Sexwise*; *Nothing But the Girl: The Blatant Lesbian Image,* edited by Jill Posener; *The Best American Erotica Series, The Sexual State of the Union*; and her newest book on creating a personal sexual philosophy, *Full Exposure.*

Susie, who, according to the *New York Times,* has become "the avatar of American erotica with her widely published anthologies and essays, suggests that such sexual imaginings give us 'a portrait of the times we live in.' And perhaps they do, because submission and dominance, masochism and sadism, exhibitionism and voyeurism are now familiar from fashion ads and television shows and mainstream movies. The reasons for the scope of recent erotic obsessions are familiar: a confluence of political and social changes, an insatiable quest for ever larger audiences for pop entertainment and academic absorption in the subjects of body and gender. But the preoccupations are also more evident because of the dissolving boundaries between the public and the private in American life. Erotica and porn, once so private that collections were hidden in back rooms, have become aggressively public," the *Times* article concludes.

Susie has a regular column in the on-line magazine Salon.com and continues writing fiction and essays.

Susie is smart, articulate, funny, and infinitely entertaining in her very unconventional way.

## An Unconventional Woman

If a woman asserts her sexual interests in her life, does that mean that she will never get to be a wife or a mother—that she's sort of thrown away the blue ribbon of virtue even though there are no modern women who think that they should be barefoot and pregnant? I think there are some real old-fashioned messages that are entrenched, and you're encouraged to think, "Oh, well, *of course,* you can get a degree, you can have a fancy job, and you can be articulate in politics, but for God's sake don't act like a whore." In other words, don't assert your sexual interest. Don't talk about your desire. Don't be honest with yourself sexually. Stay in that kind of self-hating, ignorant place where women's magazines would like you to stay for the rest of your life. Then maybe you'll be somebody's trophy; won't that be sweet? It's really gross.

I'm bisexual, and I've lived with a man, who is my primary partner, for ten years now. But I learned from my lesbian life that within the lesbian world, a notion of one's virtue of making you worthy as a life partner is irrelevant.

Women don't choose women because they think you've been around and you're used goods. That wouldn't even come up in a lesbian relationship. Virginity, being chaste, and being a good girl aren't part of the sexual dance. Lesbians have a lot of ideas about what it means to be a good partner and be loving or be noble. It's not like anything goes, but that's something that doesn't have a place because there is no proprietary value in having a girlfriend. Girlfriends are not your property. So it doesn't matter what the perceived virtue or trophy-esqueness of them is. Maybe your girlfriend's really cute, and that makes you proud. Or she particularly excels at cooking or sports or something else, but it doesn't have that kind of property value that marriage has always had underlying it. That's a lesson that you don't have to eat pussy to understand. It doesn't have to do with the sex act. It has to do with your consciousness and putting on a be-free in your mind. About being a woman.

I was exploring those themes in early theater shows and writings I was doing. Out of the blue, I got a fan letter—my first fan letter—from a woman who'd heard me at a poetry reading. She said that she and her buddy were starting an entertainment magazine for the adventurous lesbian, called *On Our Backs,* and that just made me burst out laughing. I had read *Off Our Backs,* the feminist newspaper, for years. It was the hard-core feminist journal for people who thought *Ms.* was just dandelion fluff. When the sex wars started happening, men were on the wrong side of that—so conservative—just as bad as Phyllis Schafly. To call something *On Our Backs*—I just loved that. I immediately got the idea of it, the chicness of saying that one can appear to be in a submissive position and yet still be calling the shots, that sexuality is not this thing that's so literal where if you're lying on the floor, that means that you don't have any power. That's not what it's like with sex. I just loved that, so I said, "Yes. Yes, I want to write. I want to sweep the floor. [This was before computers.] I want to do everything."

Our reason for doing this was that it was our own little private backlash to a certain conservative wing in the lesbian movement that we had been chafing against. You have to have a certain kind of haircut, certain kind of clothes, certain kind of sex; you have to eat a certain kind of food. Screw them! We're gonna do something that's gonna make them so mad! It was really rebellious. In hindsight, it was the trumpet sounds of the first queer generation gap. Even though the women who started *On Our Backs* were all technically boomers, right on the cusp, it was a new way of thinking about feminism and sexuality. We didn't want to do things the way our feminist moms or older sisters would have done. It was that kind of a changing of the guard. It was also the kind of influence that gay men had had with their sexual vision; it influenced a lot of urban lesbians. Can one have a sexually communal feeling? Does everything have to be monogamous? Or do friendship and loyalty exist on different levels? Can we play with sex more, or do we have to fall in love with the first person we have an orgasm with? There was a huge influence from the gay men's scene. It's so poignant. This was just before AIDS was understood. Here lesbians were taking the baton and running with it on a fierce level, with all that feminist interest in explaining everything and debating everything and going over and over it in therapeutic detail. *On Our Backs* ended up really changing lesbian culture and what people thought of it.

You write something, and everyone's going to be curious about you. It was just like being an artist in any other sense of the word where you attracted attention to yourself, to your work, if you were popular. So I started experiencing this, "Oh, who's Susie Bright? Who's Susie Sexpert?" This alter-ego was coming up when I started doing the advice column. Susie Sexpert wasn't quite me. She's much sassier and bitchier than I would ever really be in my life and much more confident than I am. I started getting more attention. Then someone from a men's magazine that doesn't exist anymore, *Penthouse Forum,* called me. Actually it was a magazine that a lot of women read too. It was mostly letters and quasi-educational articles about where the clitoris is and that fantasies are OK. They gave it the college try by having experts write stories. The guy who called said he really liked my writing in *On Our Backs* and would I like to write a column on porn every month. I was like, "Yeah, sure." It paid enough that I could quit my job with Good Vibrations. I didn't know that much about porn, but I could find out. This was before VCRs really became ubiquitous. I was sitting in theaters and watching these adult movies all day, and really trying to do a crash course in what was going on. I was talking to people and learning as much about the business as I could.

Meanwhile at *On Our Backs,* we decided to make sex videos because there was nothing that portrayed lesbians in anything that we would recognize as realistic. Everybody in the typical girl-girl porn movies, which is what I call them to differentiate them from the lesbian-made movies with girl-girl scenes, had long fingernails and big hair; there were always fems and fems together. Very often in those days there was a softer, more tender thing, focused on cunnilingus. That's changed because of those movies we made. We wanted to show women who are androgynous and butch as well as fems. We wanted realistic hands and hair. Lesbians' hands are very important because they're used a lot for penetration. We're going to show all different kinds of fucking. That's what the lovers were into. Yes, oral sex, too, but that didn't define the sex act.

Our movies didn't fit into any normal category, and the regular porn business was puzzled over us. What are you *doing*? We didn't know. We just got our friends who were willing to fuck on camera to do it. That was it. We barely knew where the on button was for the camera, but we were enthusiastic, and we wanted authenticity. We wanted to capture some hot couples on camera. It had a huge impact on the lesbian image and, later, on porn in general. Meanwhile I'm writing reviews and really enjoying making a living this way.

In the beginning, I was like anybody else. I was in my late twenties and had never seen a porn movie before—typical for most women of my generation. Many conventions of porn I was puzzled by. I felt as if I wanted to tug on someone's sleeve and say, "I don't understand. How come the guys are all coming on the outside? What's that?" There's a certain way positions were shown that puzzled me. On the other hand, the more movies I saw, the more I realized that pornography was much more diverse and maverick and eccentric than entertainment mediums that are more legitimate, like television or Hollywood movies.

People say, "You've seen one, you've seen them all." Not true. Most people wouldn't say that about Hollywood or TV, but Hollywood and TV are much more homogeneous than pornography. In pornography, you have all kinds of different bodies and faces that would never fly in any other mainstream entertainment because they're made cheaply and by people who are such mavericks. They think, "I know this is a sex movie, but I'm going to have my own special message," or "I'm going to have my own little thing that maybe nobody understands except me, but I don't care. I can do what I want." You find a really wild array of personal expression going on in porn.

When porn became attacked by feminists like Andrea Dworkin and Catherine McKinnon and was sort of put under a political magnifying glass, there were so many attacks about violence in pornography. There were successful prosecutions of these themes in movies. The people who run this industry are like the people who run all the other industries—not artists thinking about how to be avant-garde, cutting edge. They don't ask, "What can we do to really change the world?" No. It's about money. These guys are conservative old fuddy-duddies who don't want their wives or daughters making these movies either. They're not worse than anybody else, but they're not bohemians. They reacted by taking all the dramatic qualities out of porn, which made porn, in the beginning of the video age, much more boring because people would stay away from the kind of conflicts you would usually see in a plot because they didn't want to be accused of violence or of having depressing or degrading themes. If we pulled out the paper and looked at all the movies playing right now, I'm sure there would be themes of struggle, conflict, melancholy, tragedy. Those were censored completely out of pornography. The X-rated people are not going to be the ones to make a beautifully scripted and acted, quality, invigorating movie. They're not going to do it, and Hollywood's not going to do it. It's going to be somebody who's coming in from the cold, trying to use some qualities of those businesses to get their message out.

I learned a lot about behind the scenes. That was probably what a lot of people are interested in. I immediately felt sympathetic since I was kind of in the sex business myself, ever since I'd worked at Good Vibrations. I knew the judgments that people have about you, number one, you're stupid, and two, that you're abused. There's a camaraderie in the porn world;

in a way, we don't have casting couches in porn. When you fuck, you get paid to fuck. The rest of the time you're treated like a professional and an individual. Porn people are proud of that. They think Hollywood is sleazy and creepy and disingenuous and that the pornographers are the honest crowd. Not that there aren't screwballs everywhere; they're not a bunch of saints. But probably the biggest problem behind the scenes in porn isn't the kind of stereotypical nightmare that people are being raped and tortured. That's not the tragedy. The tragedy is the stigma and the sense that what I'm doing is something that people will say, "You wasted your life. Does your family still love you anymore? Can you have a family?" That sense of being outcast, much like queer people felt outcast before Stonewall.

So when people bring up the problems in pornography, I ask, "Do you mean compared to Warner Brothers? Compared to the NBA? I don't think so."

The thing about my thirties is that I became a mom. That changed everything. There's a story with it. I had fallen crazy in lust-love with this guy, and after years of being with a woman, it was so novel, so wild, and just felt so taboo and exciting. The first time I went to bed with him, he started rhapsodizing about what a beautiful baby we would make together. I was like, "Wow! This is how he talks dirty. It's kind of arousing. Damn!" Procreation has been separate from sex for me for so long. It's just so easy. I was very touched by it. Even when I had been with men before, no one ever talked about having children. Never, never, never, never.

He was a total Casanova; millions of girls were in a tizzy all over town, and he was quite cruel. He didn't have any friends, just victims. But his beauty, his charm, and his unusual sensitivities could be intoxicating. I got pregnant for the first time with him, when I was twenty-nine. I had an abortion. It was so embarrassing: I was Susie Sexpert, and I hadn't been with a man in so long that the whole concept of birth control seemed like a distant concern. I depended on him to use condoms, and him being him, he was undependable.

Once upon a time I had been the girl in high school who handed out birth control directions and pamphlets to the others. I never came even close to getting pregnant in my teenage years, even though I had a very busy sex life. Here I was almost thirty, and I got pregnant for the first time. It was very humbling.

I had an abortion. I came home from the abortion and had this epiphany. I was *so* relieved. You know when you're first pregnant, you feel like aliens are taking over your body and I was, "It's gone. I'm me again."

I remember when I was a teenager, waiting for my period to come. I had a very late period. And they said, "When your period comes, you will feel like a woman." My period came, and it was like, "Shit, I'm going to be late for school." I did not feel like a woman. It was just a pain in the ass. But this moment after the abortion, I had the *I'm a woman* feeling. I was just like, "Wow, me! I could have a baby." After that point, I would have private fantasies about a little girl and me. In the fantasies she was already talking, about six or seven years old; it wasn't a baby. I never fantasized about babies. I didn't know anything about babies. I never babysat babies.

Meanwhile I separated from my woman lover I'd been with for many years. I was single. When you've been with someone six years, you're like, "Pinch me. What's next?" I still had a soft spot in my sexual feelings for the man I was just telling you about. I hadn't seen him in months. One night I was ovulating, and I just went over to his house. I was just as mysterious as he was. If I'd said, "I'm ovulating, and I really want to get pregnant," he would have slammed the door in my face. Even though he has knocked up hundreds of women, he's always got to be romantic. He can't ever address anything straight on. He's not the kind of person you could sit down and say, "I'd really like you to donate your sperm." I want somebody who won't be involved but would be happy to get me pregnant. That's essentially what he ends up doing, but he can't handle being told that. It offends him. So I was like, "Hi, can I come in?" Like teenagery. Like I just happened to be in the neighborhood. We made love, and I was quite sure, from the moment he came inside me, that I was pregnant. I just scampered off. It was so unconscious, like when somebody else is running the controls. When can I test? At first I got a negative and I was, "Shit." That was when I said, "Why am I so angry? I really want to be pregnant, don't I?" Then I got the positive. Then I rushed over to his place and said, "I'm having a baby. I don't want anything from you except for you to acknowledge paternity. Would that be OK? Great. Fine. that's all I want."

Then the pregnancy began. A lot of people think I'm the changeling in my family history. "What do your parents think of you? This must be so outrageous." I realized in my thirties that it was my mother who changed the role of what women did in her family history. The women in her Irish-Catholic family stayed married unhappily all their lives, lived in incredible poverty, had many, many children, and died young. My mom went to college and got a higher degree and was married. But as soon as she had me, she divorced my father and raised me herself, and never married again. She was never attracted to drinking (that was another big theme in her family: alcoholism). She didn't do any of those things. She changed some of the biggest things you can change: single motherhood, one child, a lot of education, and no patriarch in the family. I'm so much like her. I got pregnant at the same age that she got pregnant with me. I didn't bother getting married, so that was a change, but it's closer to her than to anybody else.

When I thought about getting ready to have the baby, I was so surprised by all the conservative questions people would ask me. Their concern about the father being there. I thought that I'm close to my dad now, and when I was a kid, I'd see him on school holidays, and he paid child support and alimony. He did not raise me on a daily basis, but he loved me tremendously. It was a sort of an old-fashioned divorce. When people asked, "Are you worried about there not being a man around?" I said no. If I had to share this with somebody and we had to argue over what we were going to do, I'd go out of my mind. How do people do it? How do people negotiate parenthood? I'm going to do this, and we're going to do that, and bedtime and TV. *I decide it. Me.* I don't have to discuss it with anybody. That made me actually look at people who were raising children together and think, "I'm impressed. I couldn't do it." It felt natural. I don't remember my parents being married. I just remember me and my mom. Unlike my mom, I had a number of close friends by my side constantly during my pregnancy. They started loving Aretha before Aretha started coming out of me because they just got so invested in everything being good for me.

I didn't know what I was going to be doing for my livelihood. I didn't do one of those lists where you add up the charges of how much it's going to cost to have a child and then you come up with a million dollars or something like that. I didn't do that. None of that. I did not have health insurance. Nothing. But it was going to be OK. I wasn't going to end up on the streets with my child, hungry and alone. There were too many people who care about me. There was no way that was going to happen. Once I got down to that level, then it was full steam ahead. Not everybody could handle that situation the same way, but I knew I could. Why be pitiful and pretend otherwise?

I was the first of my friends to have a baby. The young mom. Most of my friends are just starting to have babies now. Or they're still young and single, and the whole thing seems bizarre to them.

A lot of enlightenment started coming out of me that had to do with Aretha. A lot of decisions I made were about what would be best for her. Some people neglect themselves too much to sacrifice for their child, and then they feel they went too far. But that's never how it's been for me. It's always been that when we decided to move or when I was changing a relationship or what I had to do, the strong thing to protect her interest was the strongest thing I could have done for myself. I would have been too willing not to stand up for myself when I was single.

I'd think, "Thanks, Aretha, for giving me the inspiration," because now I have the habit. I know what that's like. I felt as if I learned the meaning of sacrifice. I always thought a sacrifice was something that really hurt, was really awful, but you did it because it had to be done! You just kind of bit your tongue and did it. With my child, making a sacrifice for her is like a love sacrifice; it's like, "I'm doing this for you," and I am giving out something, but just the act of doing it is so rewarding, I can't even begin to tell you. That's sacrifice. It has a certain kind of feminine quality to it that I realize comes from the mothering place. That was very moving.

This is sort of a Freudian side of things—being able to redress things that hurt you when you were a child and finally being able to say, "I suffered as a kid in a certain way, and I'm not going to do that," and I have the clarity not to do it with my kid. Some things I see myself repeating, old junk, that I wish I could nip in the bud. In my family, everybody lies about anything that's embarrassing or they're ashamed about in family history. If a question's asked on a touchy subject, you either act as if it was never said, or it just disappears, like a fart, or you get a complete falsehood as an answer. I had this thing with Aretha that has certainly affected questions about sexuality as well as money—everything: don't lie to her, no matter how frustrating it is, even if I don't know the answer. It's better to say, "I don't know," or "I'm so frustrated," or "I have mixed feelings"; she can understand that on a simple level. Most of the time, I *do* know what the truth of the matter is, and it's just maybe hard to tell. It's hard to tell her that I did love the man who is her birth father, but my love was an illusion on many levels on my part. It wasn't a love of a great friend or someone you'd even treat like family. It was great romance and a great erotic feeling, but it was a fantasy. He hurt me a lot, but I feel just as sort of guilty that I didn't know who he was. I was walking around with this thing in my head and saying, "That's you. It wasn't him." I'm sure he knew that. And he tried to tell me in his clunky way, "I am not this guy in shining armor that you've gussied up in your mind." I said, "No, no; don't tell me that; let me dream on." I didn't say that literally, but I see how it kept up.

The time will come when she has crushes and infatuations and great loves with her own peers. I want to be able, when she does and if it's somebody I think is a bounder and a cad, to be able to say, "I know what it's like to be in love with a bounder and a cad. There's something about it that's really thrilling, but it's not something that keeps you strong. You can have that kind of love, and you can respect the creative part of you that is inspired by that and that is aroused by that, but it's not the only kind of love there is." I can't wait to be able to say that. I don't want to be the kind of person who says, "You can't see him," or "Your love is stupid or wrong," which I think doesn't do anything. I also don't want to nurture false illusions, like, "Maybe he'll change some day." Not everybody's good; not everybody's bad. I want to be able to tell her that love is tricky, which she understands now. I like that. Being more honest with her is also really good for me as a writer. In terms of crafting writing, you know if you can be honest about something and come out with it in your writing, it's probably going to be really good. Rather than if you try to slip around that or quick write some little thing that skirts the issue or paints a cliché over it that maybe no one will notice. Oh, they'll notice. Sometimes when I'm writing, I'll come to an experience where I think, "Oh, I can't say this; I don't know how to say this." Then I go, "Well, what if you had to say it to Aretha. How would you say it?" "How would you tell the truth to Aretha?" has turned into, "How do you tell the truth about difficult things?" I like that too.

The other big change in my life in my thirties has been that I changed from the struggling student and artist, sleeping on the floor with the cardboard box, and had a middle-class lifestyle. I became successful in my work. Nobody else in my family works in the arts. They're artistic people, but it is just unbelievable that anybody would make their living at it. It's still a topic of great doubt and suspicion among my relatives: "What is this?" It's too late to tell me to go back to school and do something else. This is it. I've had these thrills. I moved constantly as a kid; I went to twenty-four different schools. We moved every six months to a year. Now I've settled down and I bought a home—things that aren't part of my past that I take a lot of pride and comfort and sanctuary in. I surprised myself. As a child I was a vagabond; maybe I could never live in a smaller town (I've always lived in the city). I've thought about it—that I was motivated to do those things because of Aretha. Wouldn't it be nice to live in a small place with freedom? So I have a young daughter, and I live with my partner, who has been my lover since I was pregnant, so he's been fathering Aretha. He's a friend—part of our family since the beginning. I have some weeks coming up when she's going to summer camp and he has some things to do, so I could do whatever I want without the two of them. I'm like, "What! I don't have any friends!" That's not true, of course, but I'm so used to doing everything with my family that I feel out of touch when I am away from them. I've been beside myself, trying to figure out where I shall go. What should I do if you guys aren't here and we're not organizing our plans all the time? The big excitement this summer is putting a new roof on our house and redoing the plumbing. Like Erma Bombeck, I'm in the young, home owner phase of my life! I've got a young child; I've never owned a house before;

it's got a million things wrong with it. It's like an episode out of a Dave Barry column. But I've read enough literature to know this is a phase that one leaves.

This is why this decade has been so tricky: some people did this in their twenties. I envy those forty year olds who are grandmas now because they already did it all, and they're still full of energy, bright-eyed and bushy-tailed. They're so cool; I'm exhausted. And I've only got a nine year old.

I would raise other children, and that isn't just theoretical. It's been propositioned to me on a couple of occasions, because Jon would love to have more children. But get pregnant and carry a baby again? No way. Look what happened to me the last time; I was a basket case. I had a difficult pregnancy and birth, and my health declined really severely after childbirth. I know I look big and strong as a horse, but things did not work out easily. So I'm kind of scared of it. I don't want to do that again. I feel as if it took all we had just to go through the first time and I was ten years younger.

My new book, *Full Exposure,* is about sexual creativity and erotic expression. It's an antidote to those books that promise you a better sex life with all these wacky proposals and steps. Having a great sex life is about being sexually conscious and connected inside. It's not about positions; it's not about how many lovers you have; it doesn't even matter if you're sexually active at this moment. I try to convey to people why I feel sexually tuned in and alive and sensitive. I don't make love with Jon every day—not by a long shot. I'm not masturbating up a storm. I am not watching porn movies every day. I'm not turning on all my vibrators at the same time—although I've enjoyed all kinds of things like that.

When you're a sex expert, a lot of people get angry. They say, "Well, I don't *want* to swing on a chandelier, Susie. Do you mind!" I don't. Not at all. Screw the chandelier. It's not about that. It's about a kind of comfort and pleasure in your sensuality, in your body, and appreciating your fantasies, your arousal, and your daydreams. I think creativity and sexuality are like this; they're both the same kind of thing. They pull on the unconscious; they're about risk and daydreams and contradictions, and where you'll go blind and where you draw the line. Everything that people go through in their creativity process is parallel to what they say about their sexuality. So I wanted to do a book that tried to introduce the notion that everybody has a sexual philosophy, although you've never called it that or put it down. You do. Why don't you step up to bat with it? Come conscious with it.

The further I get away from the thirties, I'll think of them as a decade when you still have a great deal of your physical power. For most women in their thirties, it's a time of tremendous physical energy and power. You couldn't be in the Olympics at this point, but you're very powerful physically and health-wise. At the same time, you're not a virgin anymore. You're not a girl anymore. Only eighty year olds are going to call you a girl when you're in your thirties. You've been around the block; you've learned something. Even if you were raised in a suburb, you begin to feel as if you can call yourself streetwise. You've loved; you've hated. You've probably had your heart broken. You are tempered a little bit by some harsh experiences, but you still have such a reserve of strength. I used to think, because of that thing about not trusting anybody over thirty, that there was a sense of being such an old fogy. Thirty is not fogy; thirty is still kicking around in the buttercups if you want to. I didn't enter my thirties knowing who I was going to be or having the reputation for anything. At the end of it, I did.

A lot of women have been valued almost entirely for their looks—being cute or adorable or precocious. As you enter your thirties, if you realize that's what it's been all about and that's how you're valued professionally or personally, well that's all going to change over this decade. You may still be a very good-looking person or be the sort of person who makes people smile and blush. It's not like all these qualities are going to be erased, but there are going to be a lot of other people who are even more adorable. You're not going to be as cute as a button anymore. Come on. You can't do that kind of precociousness and adorableness, fluffy kitty thing. Thirty is like, *Kill fluffy.* You have to start cultivating and appreciating fundamentally from the inside. You might decide you're going to do things about your maturity and your self-respect for your maturity. You may decide, "You know what? I never did invest in my education, never did become the worldly person, or never challenged myself in certain ways. I'm going to do that now." But fundamentally it will start within you, then in your personal and your family relationships of considering who you are once Little Bo Peep is out of the picture.

I don't have a before-and-after story to tell about this. I was an egghead and a bookworm when I was a kid. I wasn't particularly singled out for being cute or adorable. I was to my mommy, but that wasn't why anybody was interested in me. I envied the popular girls terribly, because I wished I could have whatever that magic was that they had, that made them so irresistible when we were young. I envied that. The older I got, the more I was doing all right, because my intellectual qualities became more and more important to people around me; they were valued. When I was in school, it was not in to be smart. But then when I got out of school, it was really important to be smart.

It's especially unpopular to be smart in grade school and high school. *How could you embarrass yourself getting an A?! Don't show anybody your report card; they'll know what a big nerd you are.* In college, it's more important to be smart than in high school, but it's still more important to be socially accepted. Then after the parade of the typical education is over, it's really important to be smart. That's when, if you have intellectual or verbal or perceptive abilities, aesthetic abilities, Wow! Then the world is very interested in those if you shine in them.

This is something I faced a little bit. I was so sheltered, and this is so weird because I became Susie Sexpert. I never understood the dirty jokes, never said a swear word because I was so sheltered before I left home. Getting to know women who worked in the sex business, I was like, Wow! Pussy really does make the world go round. I didn't know how hungry people are for sex and how much sexual power women have, and how most men would just fall down screaming to have the tiniest little bit of attention, and how people aren't looking for supermodels. Womanly women are very goddess-like. I finally got it. The women who did this as a business were like Susie, wake up. Men feel like babies when they're around us.

We hold everything. They want us. I was really noticing that. Then if that's the case, a lot of people must be finding me attractive, and I just haven't been aware of it because I have been so convinced that I'm awkward and have braces and big shoes and thick glasses and I'm a bookworm and I don't know how to be sexual and I don't know how to be charming and I'm going to trip over my shoelaces. My idea of myself was as a real oddball.

Right around my late twenties and early thirties, I turned up the volume on my sexual output. People just cleared the path for me. I'm tall, and I'm fair, and I have strong features and this statuesque body. People will lay out around me if I even consciously apply it one tiny little bit. At that point, I was like, *I wish I'd known this before.* I was so insecure. I did not realize that you don't have to be Marilyn Monroe; it isn't a movie star thing. I was wondering, How would it have been if I had known this when I was young and used it as a force on my behalf? Or would it have made me hardened? I don't know.

I didn't know one darn thing about money. I thought I was on top of the world because I knew how to balance a checkbook. I know lots of people who don't even know how to put number, date, name of company, price. ATMs for them are just one giant disaster because they never understand why everything is bouncing. They actually have the idea that they might strike it rich through some extraordinary event, like gambling or the lottery or found treasure. I was always skeptical about the lottery idea; that's just me. But it's only been at the end of my thirties that I've realized this whole work-hard thing was a working-class illusion that I was under. There are a lot of people who work like dogs all the time. Does that mean they have a lot of money? No. Your actual physical labor has nothing to do with your net worth. No one ever talked to me about saving or investing. I'm sure I've made many millions for the credit card companies.

The biggest thing I did in my thirties was to get rid of $40,000 in credit card debt. I paid it off slowly, and then when I got really serious about it, I would add up how much money I was paying them and make myself so sick and so angry about it that I just started paying it off faster. Plus I got some help from people who are financial smarty-pants. They would say, "Your debt is taking so much more away from you. This half of your earnings is going to taxes. You think you're making a dollar, but you're not making a dollar. Wouldn't it be nice to be on the other side of the equation, where your dollar is actually becoming more than a dollar instead of being the one whose cash is being dwindled into nothing?"

I'm not sure how to do this, because it was never done with me as a kid, but I want so much to share my new knowledge with my daughter. I said to her yesterday (and I'm still a babe in the woods with this), "Aretha, because you're so young, if you save your money now, you'll have so much money when you're older that you won't have to work as hard as I do. You've got time on your side. Even if you had an investment in something that didn't do so well, so what? You still have your childhood ahead of you before you even have to do anything—before it matters at all."

When I went into business, I had to file Schedule C income taxes, that is, I had to list expenses, and I'd never done that before. I learned from my two stripper friends who are my finance gurus: Save every receipt. A receipt is like money in hand. Add them all up, and you'll get money back. Think of it as money. I did. I said, "OK, Debbie, I will." It was the first time I actually had a clue about what I spent my money on. That inspired me to make a budget. After I made a budget, the owner of Good Vibrations said, "I'm going to start an IRA [individual retirement account] for you." She just put in $200 and then forgot about it. IRA? I thought. What's that?

I don't think of retirement as a time when I'm getting to go around in my little electric cart with my granny goggles. I know it's not a bedridden, end-of-the-world thing. I'm sure I'll be working at things I'm interested in as long as I live, but I won't work as hard. I don't want to work as hard *now!* And I don't want to be on the ropes about things. I think it's criminal that there's no financial education. This is one of the things I learned when I became a socialist and got class consciousness and started looking at who makes wealth in America and who works, but I never considered it in terms of class values of how we learn about taking care of ourselves and our family. Risk. What you're worth. What makes people wealthy? Nobody ever talked about what those things meant in my family. My mom never had any savings. I thought that Henry Ford had a savings account; I didn't think of it as something ordinary people had. Plus I thought a savings account was that thing at the bank that pays 2 percent. I had no idea what a CD was, or the money market, or no-risk things. This has been a giant, giant thing. It shouldn't have been a thirties experience; it should have been a teenager experience. I dug a hole so deep.

I don't know if buying a home was the best financial decision, but in some ways it gives credibility in certain kinds of situations. People think that if I own a home, I'm safer or more respectable. I think it's really an incredible experience to have control over my dwelling; it's wonderful having my own piece of land, to do what I feel like doing and make my own mistakes and express myself, to have it be mine and not feel as if it can be yanked out from under me. But it's also a burden. It scares me. It drives me to sign contracts that maybe I'm not so crazy about because I'm thinking, *Gotta keep this place going.* The way I talk about it, it sounds as if it's an orphanage. It's just a single-family house.

Jon, my partner, is a visual artist, and he teaches. In this country, there are opportunities to teach art to people who are considered disadvantaged: prisoners, the physically disabled, the mentally disabled, juvenile delinquents—anybody considered to be in a bad way. There are funds to teach them art because it's supposed to be helpful to them. It *is* helpful to them, very helpful. I consider it the high point of this country. But if it's so good for them, why isn't it great for everybody? How come all of us aren't having wonderful art classes?

I'm the moneymaker in our family. He's where I was before I got those lucky breaks. He's really talented; everyone ooos and aahs, but he has not been discovered by Oprah.

I started in a supercommunal situation; nobody was married, and nobody said they had a monogamous relationship. Everybody is loose and free, in one big circular waterbed together. I went from that to having more primary relationships with women. You may get into your ruts regarding finances and housework in these lesbian relationships, but it's not taken for granted who's doing what—who is washing dishes or who is bringing home the bacon. You find out what that is in your relationship, but there's no givens going into it.

Coming to be with Jon and being the person who is the primary bread-winner is a nontraditional structure, but I know many women in that situation in my circle. I don't feel as if I've picked people because of this; it just turned out that way. In my circle, it's the rule rather than the exception. Some of the women in that place feel much more embarrassed and weird about it than others. When it came to being with Jon, it's more noticeable. I notice him being frustrated in a masculine way; this isn't what his dad would have done. It's all about dad: wondering if his dad looks down on him or if people are assuming that he's taking advantage of me. Yet if he was the woman, no one would be asking that. Or people say to me, "You're going on a book tour? Who's taking care of your child?" They wouldn't ask him if *he* was going on a book tour. What a stupid question. He knows how different it is to be in this place from his family history. For me, it's obvious that there's an incredible privilege to being the one who makes more money, because if you want to take advantage of it the teeniest, tiniest bit, you bring such a great deal to bear. If I get a pair of shoes that aren't in the budget, who's going to tell me I couldn't? *I* brought home this paycheck; everybody get out of my way. I've never been like this, but it occurs to me how easy it is to push it. When you're the person who isn't bringing the big money, you feel embarrassed to buy an extra candy bar because you worry that you'll be seen as pushing it.

Jon and I have known each other so long, and we've been Mr. and Mrs. Teamwork as far as this house is concerned because it has all these things that need to be done. He knows how to do it all, and I don't. He knows all the boy stuff, but he also knows all the girl stuff: he builds the house *and* cleans it. I'm not allowed to do the laundry because he thinks I'll just ruin it. He's a superb cook; he's a devoted father to our daughter. He's into aesthetics on a masculine and a feminine level about the house. What would I do without that? How can I not value that?

We've been faced with the possibility of his working more hours for more money. I never was willing to say, "Do it full time," because I thought I couldn't take it if he weren't here to do this. If he felt this was the break he wanted or it would be so fulfilling, it would be different, but it hasn't been like that. It's always been just for the money. He'd rather be doing what we want to do here. I could not manage this place on my own; I'd have to have somebody who would help me keep things going. It's too big a responsibility. If I were all by myself, I'd be in a couple of rooms, not too big, for just my clothes, just my meals.

*It's a wonderful feeling to have the faith that even though I don't
know how in the world I'll put this next film together, I know I'll
figure it out. It's having faith in the process, honoring the process,
and not pressuring myself to be so brilliant as to have worked the
whole thing out before I've even started.*

LISA LEEMAN

# Lisa Leeman

## PROFILE

When I first met Lisa Leeman, she was doing preliminary work on a documentary film about turning forty, as a way of looking at midlife, which she hoped to find funding for and make. We had been introduced by a mutual friend who knew about Lisa's project and my own book, *On Women Turning 40,* and, as he suspected, we liked each other immediately. Lisa has one of the most natural and infectious laughs I've ever heard. She seems to find delight in everything, which makes it a riot being around her.

Lisa lives in Venice Beach, California, in a large bungalow one block from the beach. As a documentary filmmaker wanna be myself, I am inspired by the commitment it takes to live this lifestyle. Most of her time seems to be spent editing other people's documentaries and teaching young filmmakers in the prestigious film department at the University of Southern California. Lisa has made three documentary films herself, as well as edited almost a dozen for fellow independent filmmakers, and she is currently fundraising for her fourth film.

Her first film, *Metamorphosis: Man into Woman,* premiered at the Sundance Film Festival in 1990, winning the Filmmakers Trophy. An intimate

**53**

portrait of a transsexual undergoing a sex change, the film follows a man becoming a woman over a three-year period, as a way to look at gender roles. *Metamorphosis* raises profound questions about contemporary gender roles as Gary's fantasies collide with the realities of living as a woman. Watching Gary/Gabby make conscious choices of what is appropriate and inappropriate behavior for a woman today challenges audiences to confront personal biases and expectations of what we think men and woman are supposed to be.

Lisa describes her second film, *Breaking Up,* as a comic video diary of the aftermath of a romance. Her third film, *Fender Philosophers,* was a look at popular culture and self-expression. It's a portrait of Americans: of who we are and what we care about, as seen through (of all things) our bumper stickers.

True to the two themes that consistently show up in Lisa's work, gender roles and popular culture, she is now fundraising for her fourth film, which continues her exploration into gender roles by examining the thriving mail-order-bride business. She hopes to follow several American men as they use the mail-order-bride business to seek "an old-fashioned wife" from the Philippines.

Lisa still has time for regular kayaking trips and yoga. Romance is a sometimes elusive element in her life. And along with her passion for documentary filmmaking, she would like to extend her passion to a committed relationship. Her enthusiasm and inspiration as an artist and for the artist's life are palpable, and Lisa is articulate in her expression about them.

## Metamorphosis

My greatest happiness is the love I've known in my life, and my greatest sorrow is that my last relationship didn't work out. No, my greatest sorrow is that I didn't visit a friend and coteacher before he died of cancer at the age of forty-six. I've learned not to take time for granted and to do things I need to do, no matter how uncomfortable it might be. I'd advise any woman (any person) who has passions unacted on to go for it; just do it; carpe diem—all slogans that have become advertising campaigns. But when it comes right down to it, it's that simple. Most of all, don't let fear or inexperience or lack of money or even lack of time stop you. Fear is the worst barrier.

To those just starting out to follow their passion, I'd say, "Don't be afraid to ask for help, for knowledge and how-to. I've found that if you are genuinely passionate about manifesting your vision and have done your homework, people are incredibly generous with their time. Find a community of supportive people, whether it's a writers' group, or painting class, or documentary film work-in-progress screenings, or whatever." It can be very isolating to do creative work on your own. Even writing, which by its nature is solitary work, needs an audience, and feedback during the writing process keeps me going. I've also found it helpful to read interviews with men and women who've done whatever it is I'm aspiring to do. They usually talk a lot about being afraid and being anxious about not knowing the outcome of their work, but they forge ahead anyway. That gave me permission not to wait until my fear went away, not to wait until I felt I'd solved every problem ahead of time. Of course, some of this comes with age; I've made three films and edited almost a dozen, and it's a wonderful feeling to have the faith that even though I don't know how in the world I'll put this next film together, I know I'll figure it out. It's having faith in the process, honoring the process, and not pressuring myself to be so brilliant as to have worked the whole thing out before I've even started!

I'm an independent documentary filmmaker. That means I come up with an idea, do the research, do the fundraising, find the crew, keep fundraising, direct the shooting of the film, do more fundraising, direct the editing of the film, and then am responsible for getting the film out into the world. I usually look for a coproducer because I like to collaborate, and frankly, it can get lonely and overwhelming to produce a film on your own for three or four or five years. I got my B.A. in filmmaking and have been doing it ever since.

I've made three documentary films of my own over the last ten years, which they say is considered successful for an independent filmmaker, but it feels so sloooowww to me. The hardest part of independent filmmaking is the struggle to raise the money (and to support myself while I'm doing it). The biggest reward is when I've made the film I've set out to make, and feel an audience react to the film and be moved and understand what it is I set out to say or explore in the film.

Every January I go to the Sundance Film Festival; I've missed only one year in the last fifteen. The festival has gotten overcrowded and more hyped and more Hollywoodesque, but I still go to be inspired by the new documentaries I see there each year. I stay six or seven days and see three or even four films a day. It's incredibly inspiring to see good new work, strong content passionately expressed, new forms, and the fierce commitment of the filmmakers. It regenerates and reinspires me for the coming year. I'm also very sentimental about Sundance because my first film, *Metamorphosis,* premiered there and won an award that year. And several other films I've edited have been in the competition, with one film winning another award. Last year I was honored by being invited to be a judge on the documentary jury, which was really fun. It made it easier to see all sixteen documentaries in competition.

Awards are a funny thing for a filmmaker. I believe you have to make the films you want and need to make; you shouldn't make films hoping for awards, or fame, and fortune (especially in documentary!). That said, independent filmmaking can be a hard path, and getting that recognition from peers is just plain validating. There's no way around that. The key is to keep your vision and goals clear and know why you really made that film.

For me, filmmaking is a way to express myself, to explore issues I'm wondering about, to jog people's minds, to show something or someone to the world in a new way. It's a way of communicating with large audiences about a message or even just a question. I joke that my films are sideways social issue films; they're not overtly ideological or about causes, though I'm moved by political films and feel they have an important place in our culture. The films I'm drawn to make are about relationships, people, gender roles, self-expression.

Why do I make documentaries, which seem a marginal form in the shadow of Hollywood and don't pay too much? I believe in the power of the form, to entertain, to educate, to persuade, and, maybe most important, to open minds and hearts, to touch souls in a way that many fiction films can't do. To introduce the peoples of our world to each other. On a more personal level, I also have my reasons. There were a lot of secrets in my family when I was growing up, and making documentaries is a way for me to shape my own truth about the world around me. Ideas for films come to me all the time. Ideas are a dime a dozen! The trick is to pick my projects carefully. I have to make sure I can live with a film for a few years if that's what it takes to raise the money and make the film. My first film took four years to research, fund, and produce. Sometimes I'm halfway through a film when I realize the personal impetus behind making it. For example, *Metamorphosis* follows a man for three years as he undergoes a sex change. It's a very unsensational, very intimate portrait of Gary slowly blossoming into Gabby, the person he always saw himself as. (The pronouns get tricky!)

I'd always been interested in gender roles. When I got out of film school, someone loaned me Renee Richards's autobiography *Second Serve*. Renee's book is fascinating; she was born as a man and grew up convinced that he was really a female trapped in a man's body. The book chronicles his struggles to become the person he believed him- or herself to be. I thought a portrait of a transsexual's journey from man to woman would be incredible. What could be more visual than a man becoming a woman?! Plus the story implicitly raises questions of what we as a society think men and women should be. I spent a year researching the subject, reading every autobiography I could find and going to weekly support groups for transsexuals and transvestites. I found a coproducer, and we raised money little by little and shot over a period of three years.

Somewhere in the middle of making the film, I realized why I was personally drawn to the subject. I've always been happy being a woman, but when I was young, I rejected a lot of traditional roles and behavior for women, and by my late twenties, when I was making this film, I was starting to integrate some of what I'd rejected into my life. Small things like wearing makeup, which I'd never bothered with and which represents a woman's role as beauty object (my mother had always put a big emphasis on looks); and I was asking myself what behavior is innately feminine and what is socialized. I found myself making a film where someone was consciously picking and choosing how to be a woman. I watched Gabby struggle with the same issues many "genetic girls" (as the transsexuals would call us) grappled with. In fact, I watched many transsexuals working to acquire the very traits and behaviors that many naturally born women had worked hard to unravel: being passive, quiet, deferring, unassertive; needing external—and male—attention to feel validated as a woman; and so on.

It would get surreal sometimes. I'd show up at a shoot wearing shorts and high-top sneakers, and Gabby would open the door in a flowing dress, look me up and down, and say, "Well, aren't you dressed like a man today?" Gabby would flounce around work in a miniskirt, and her coworkers (the women) would complain that she was trying to become a Barbie doll. But what I observed is that when a transsexual goes through a sex change as an adult, the person still needs to go through that adolescent trial and error to test the new role as a woman, but he or she is living and acting out that adolescence at thirty or forty or fifty years old, and it can get confusing for everyone involved. When I started making that film, I was convinced that femininity and masculinity are mostly social constructs, but by the time I finished the film, I gave a lot more credit to our hormones for defining male and female behavior. In a way, we all go through a metamorphosis of our own.

*Metamorphosis* was well received, and it won the Filmmakers Trophy when it premiered at the Sundance Film Festival in 1990. It was broadcast on PBS's prestigious series *POV* and has been broadcast and screened around the world. The *New York Times* reviewer wrote that the film "subtly raises intriguing questions about the very definition of being a woman. The resulting portrait has reverberations within reverberations." That review made me so happy, because I felt that I'd done what I set out to do: I made a compelling portrait film and succeeded in getting audiences to question our assumptions about gender stereotypes. In fact, the film is screened a lot in university classes in women's studies, as well as in classes in psychology, sociology, and sexuality. After the film was on PBS, we got letters from people who said that they used to think that transsexuals were the work of the devil, and now that they'd seen the film, they felt differently and wished Gabby the best. I was ecstatic to feel the power of the medium of film to open people's minds and foster more tolerance and acceptance. What a great form to work in!

After *Metamorphosis,* I decided I wanted to edit some documentaries to understand documentary structure better. That was the start of a parallel career that I've had for the last ten years: cutting other people's independent documentaries and continuing to make my own films. Editing has been a way to support myself during the long periods that I'm not working on my own films, and I've been privileged to edit some powerful indie documentaries, about subjects ranging from middle-class homeless women to death and dying, from families without fathers to teenage cowgirls to a film about the effect on kids of California's anti-immigration Proposition 187.

My second film came about sort of as an accident. I was going through a painful breakup of a relationship, and one day I just picked up my camera and started shooting. My soon-to-be ex-boyfriend was moving to another state for a job and wanted to call it quits. It was easier for me to go to his good-bye party behind a camera; it was easier to shoot our last times together with a camera in my hand as he packed. After he left, I was having a really hard time, and somewhere deep inside myself, I knew my grief was out of proportion to that relationship—that I was grieving things from my past that I had not resolved. So I decided to make a film about breaking up. As I say in the film, I was off on an emotional archeological dig to discover why I was having such a hard time over this breakup.

I'd always been inspired by first-person films by filmmakers like Ross McElwee and Alan Berliner who shot their lives over time and narrated their films with self-deprecating and brutally honest writing. (It's interesting that most of the early first-person films I know of were done by men, not women, though women certainly caught up in the 1980s.) The specificity of those films made them absolutely universal. So I decided to try that with this film and also to make it funny.

I'd always wondered why it is that couples who treat each other with great respect when they're together often change their behavior drastically after they've broken up, by being rude and uncaring, for example. I don't stop caring about someone I've been involved with, and this difference was driving me crazy. I put ads in the paper asking for breaking-up stories and got a big response. I videotaped ten people's stories, thinking their stories would be the spine of the film and the footage of my life would be the interstitial material. But to my surprise, it turned out just the opposite. In the editing, my story, which covered six months, became the spine of the film, and the interviews with others became a sort of Greek chorus. So what started out as not a film at all but rather a sort of coping mechanism turned into a little cathartic personal project, and then became a film that has shown in seven countries across Europe. The irony is that I haven't been able to raise money to finish an English version for the film, so it's never been seen in my own country. But I'm glad I made it, and it truly was a cathartic way to deal with emotional turmoil and turn it into a vehicle for exploration and expression. I mean, who hasn't been miserable over a breakup at some point?

My third film was entirely different. It's called *Fender Philosophers* and is about the people behind (or in front of) their bumper stickers. It's really a portrait of Americans—of who we are and what we care about—as seen through our bumper stickers. My crew and I traveled all over the West, interviewing people who are passionate about their bumper stickers and the topics of their stickers. It was one of the most fun films I've worked on and also inspiring. These are people who are often activists and want to communicate their beliefs in this incredibly populist way. I'd had the idea for years after I saw a few trucks in the 1980s that had bumper stickers that said, "No Fat Chicks." I wondered who would put that on their car, and why! Ironically, there are over 250 bumper stickers in the documentary, but we never saw that sticker. So I'm still wondering.

I'm currently fundraising to make a documentary on the mail-order-bride business, which is thriving in the United States today. I want to follow three couples—American men and Filipina women—as they look for their dream mate, correspond, meet and marry, and begin their lives together. I think the film is a way to look at the gender gap today. Many of the men speak of their discomfort or distaste for modern American women and say they want to find "an old-fashioned wife." The women speak of wanting to better their situation and say that they hear American men treat women well. The American men are looking for more traditional women, and the Filipina women are looking for more liberated men, and they're finding each other across the ocean. There is usually a definite power imbalance in these marriages, at least initially, and there are cases of abuse, and I don't want to skirt that, but I'm hoping to find three couples who will allow me into their lives to film their courtships, and whose stories will reflect the themes I'm interested in.

This film is clearly an extension of my exploration of gender roles and of a gender gap that I think still exists today. And it's easy for me to understand my interest in this now. Not only is it a compelling story, with themes that the public and I are interested in—gender roles and the expectations men and women have of each other—but it also has a resonance for me at this time of my life. I'm also feeling ready for and am looking for a committed relationship and am exploring the incredible rewards feminism has given to women, and also wondering at the price some of us have paid in trying to balance work and love.

As I enter my forties [next year], I'm conscious of wanting, even needing, to rebalance my life. I spent my twenties and thirties learning to commit to my work and passionately devoted to making films, as well as nurturing friendships and loving relationships in my life. I still feel passionate about making films and of the power of documentary film to move people and open minds and hearts, but I'm finding that I need to rebalance the time and energy I give to my work, to make more room for other parts of life. I think maybe I've proved to myself that I am a filmmaker, and now I can relax about that, and tend to other parts of myself that I did not need to nurture as much in my twenties and thirties. I find I'm craving being outside a lot, and nesting more, and thinking more about the long-term future—all just a natural evolution as one ages. I've taken up kayaking, which gives me great joy, and a totally different sense of self-sufficiency than I get in the rest of my life.

When I'm editing someone else's documentary, I try to get up early enough to meditate and take a walk before I go to work. I have recurring insomnia, so sometimes it's hard for me to get up early enough to walk on the beach, even though I live only a block away. When I'm working for myself, I give myself more time to nurture my body and soul. I take long bike rides along the beach in the morning and go to yoga classes two or three times a week. My yoga teacher is a beautiful spiritual woman who makes each class a spiritual journey, opening our hearts as we open our bodies. I've realized over the years that I've built up a lot of (needed) protective defenses when I was younger, and I need to work to keep the channels open, so I do a lot of that sort of thing: yoga, meditating, writing in my journal. I need a lot of social contact and see good friends on weekends and maybe during the week. I'm making a conscious effort to spend more time with myself, to not fill up my schedule so completely. I've learned I need more free, unstructured time to grow as a person and as an artist.

I don't see my parents too often; my father lives in Maine, on the other side of the country. My mother and I have had a rocky relationship, so we see each other in spurts. I spend Christmas with my sister and her husband and their daughter; that time together sustains me, as they usually live abroad. I spend a lot of time with friends. My friends are like my extended (sometimes my primary) family. I have one girlfriend who has been my best friend since high school and a close circle of friends from film school days in college. It's like coming home again, just getting together and yakking over dinner and a bottle(s!) of wine. And of course, I've made good friends over the years. I seem to have different communities of friends: film friends, Buddhist circle friends, kayaking friends, friends from where I teach at USC. I love it when they overlap, but in any case, they seem to fill different parts of me.

There's definitely a place for romantic love in my life, and sometimes that place is filled and sometimes it's empty. I've done the serial monogamy thing for many years. I've always liked being in a relationship with a man, even though there's stress in balancing work and a lover. I often feel that I must make a continual set of compromises, alternately choosing between time spent on work and with a lover. I have to make a conscious choice to let go of working that day and to spend it with my boyfriend, or vice versa, to decide that I need to continue working, even when I'd rather drift through a day with my boyfriend. I think being in relationship is a lifelong project.

I've always needed role models. I've had a few role models in women older than me who are filmmakers, who have balanced filmmaking, marriage, and children. I still haven't figured out how they do it, but just knowing they do makes it possible. Also, the women I've worked with seem to have a more holistic approach to filmmaking, integrating it into their lives, with studios in their homes and kids or elderly relatives around. I've started to realize I need some new role models—women closer to my own age who are now considering having a child and figuring out how to balance that with their work. I'm sure that as I get older, I'll feel a need to know and watch women age with grace, how they handle menopause, and so on, but that's a ways ahead.

So far, every year seems to get better. I remember that when I turned thirty-five, I was driving around L.A., and I started to compose my will mentally—and also thought how odd that was. So far, getting older has meant being wiser, more confident, living deeper (soulfully, spiritually), taking more risks. That's all good. I don't think much about the distant future; I haven't thought much about growing older. I'd like to be like one of those sexy, mature, wise women I've met over the years. And then when I'm really old, to be like Imogene Cunningham, the photographer who kept taking pictures into her nineties, a smart, sparky little old lady. I've always loved my birthdays. I've never understood friends who want to (and do) disappear around their birthdays. I love seeing all my friends together, and, I'll admit it, I love being feted. I've also had birthday parties where I bought dozens of flowers for the house or café, and then gave them to my friends as they left.

On my last birthday I was sad and felt very single and bereft of the man from whom I had recently separated. But I had a wonderful party. I invited friends to bring something creative to share—a song, a poem, a reading—and people were really creative. A composer friend recorded a satirical tape about aging, and two friends wrote and read poems. Now I think much more about death. As a way to stare death in the face, I deliberately took a job editing a documentary about a man dying of liver cancer. Filmmaking is such a good way to explore issues in life and to communicate with others about such deep stuff.

I went through a stage where I had many nightmares about dying, and one dream in which I actually died and drifted away. It had all the sensations of dying. I've read a lot of books about death and dying, and have temporarily found some peace about it. But I still find myself looking with fascination and some fear when I see an elderly and obviously ill person being wheeled along by a nurse. I think I'm more afraid of being ill and infirm and losing my mind than I am of dying. I figure, once you're dead, you're dead, and then I won't care any more about things I'd be missing.

I've become very interested in midlife as a developmental stage: how people deal with it in healthy ways, as well as the clichéd midlife crisis. I want to make a film about this and am still figuring out how to do it. I think it's very important to have friends older than yourself—positive role models who are sanely, richly, exuberantly living life as they get older. I'm teaching with a group of filmmakers about ten years older than me, and I am grateful to be around a bunch of people who share their wisdom with me and just to have an idea of what's ahead.

The most important lessons I've learned in life are that love and forgiveness are the highest things I can aspire to. I don't just mean romantic love; I mean soul opening, soul baring, and loving deeply your family, your friends, your lover, your community—all sentient beings. I'm not always there. I still have a hard time with forgiveness and really keeping life's calluses rubbed down, to what Buddhists call "tender heart"—a raw heart open to the joy and pain of life. The Buddhist monk and teacher Thich Nhat Hanh says that we may fall short of our aspirations, but it's good to aim for them.

I don't spend a lot of time thinking about success. I do think about what it takes for me to be happy. I'm happiest when I'm making a film I want to make and have got the funding for it, so that I can focus on doing the best work I can and am not having to stretch myself too thin by working a day job and making my film in my other time. Society undervalues documentary filmmakers (and artists in general), so when I get a grant to do my work, it makes me happy that society is supporting this work. I guess success is doing the work you want to do, being good at it, that the work is meaningful, and that it communicates to an audience, and changes them in some way.

There are tons of things I haven't done that I still wish to do. I want to make at least ten more documentary films. I want to go kayaking in the San Juan Islands. I want to go sailing in the tropics. I want to fall deeply in love and have the courage to commit myself and to get married. It'd be nice to win an Oscar for best documentary. Win the lottery. I want to learn to speak three other languages fluently. I want to deepen my meditation practice. I want to make peace in my heart and soul with my parents. I want to drink more champagne, eat more raspberries and nectarines and filet mignon. I want to go to Tibet. I want to take a year off and travel the world, and read some of the great novels I've never gotten around to. I'm sure I'm forgetting about a hundred of my other life goals. And I'm still on the fence about having children.

My thirties have been a time when I came to know myself better, to take my work more seriously, when I committed to my work, and when I first started thinking about mortality. I've always been haunted by existential angst, but the glimmers of mortality came up in my late thirties. Most of my women friends have gone through the same growth during their thirties. A few got married; several moved away from Los Angeles.

Each year has gotten better.

I have learned to love my body, and it's a love that is hard won.
Although my own body image issues have helped me to understand
women with eating disorders, they have caused me undue pressure
and pain. I have experienced internal and external pressure to be
thinner; both rage tyranny on our souls. We are plagued with a
media-imposed image of beauty—an image that only 1 percent of
women even have the genetic predisposition to achieve. Yet we have
a whole culture striving to acquire it.

FRANCESCA FERRENTELLI

# Francesca Ferrentelli

## PROFILE

Francesca Ferrentelli was born in St. Louis, where for the first five years of her life she lived with her mother, father, sister, brother, and maternal grandparents in their three-family flat in the Central West End. Above them lived her godmother, her Aunt Dolly, and various cousins, who took turns renting the third floor. The house next to them was occupied by three other households of her extended family. Altogether there were six families of related Sicilians living side by side. Her memories of that early childhood are happy ones: "We had a small above-ground pool in our blacktop of a backyard. On any given day, the yard was filled with cousins who did and didn't live on Nina Place, laughing, screaming, and playing in the pool. Every Sunday the whole brood gathered for dinner at my grandmother's; other times meals were served just where one happened to be at the time. Not much advance planning—you just ate where you were. Very communal. I loved it! It was a joyous time for all of us. To this day, when we're together, all the cousins still talk about those days on Nina Place."

As a first-generation Sicilian American and devoted Catholic, Francesca has endless colorful stories about those early years that have informed the rest of her life. Listening to her is almost like watching a movie; *Household Saints* comes to mind. Her sister, Lala, to whom she remains close, was born when Francesca was eleven and a half months old, but since Lala was three weeks premature, she didn't come home right away. This was a very stressful time for Francesca. When her mother and sister did come home, she remembers being transferred from her "pink canopy crib in her parents' room to a plain blue vinyl crib" in her grandmother's room. She was walking and talking very young, and still has memories of excited people scurrying about attending to the "present," as her mother, who was the "quintessential queen of spin," referred to Lala. But Francesca remained suspicious.

Consequently, she spent a lot of time with her grandmother, Sadi. Together they went to mass nearly every morning. They sat along the side of the church near the stations of the cross: her grandma prayed the rosary beads; she took in the sights. The images of the fallen Christ and the crucified Christ were very disturbing to her. So when she got big enough to climb onto the kitchen cabinets, she would take him down from the crucifix and lay him to nap in her doll bed. Her grandma "always got stressed up over this" and came to retrieve him, but it seemed perfectly natural to Francesca.

Her grandmother's sister, Clara, had a beauty shop in her home and, since her grandmother was a bottle blonde, they made frequent visits. Her great-grandmother, Nana Margarita, lived there too; her room, a dark chamber filled with burning candles, statues, and relics, simultaneously frightened and intrigued the children. "Face it," Francesca said in her frank and humorous manner, "that old Sicilian Catholicism is very pagan, with the Blessed Mother, the relics, and a whole pantheon of saints. That version appealed to me."

Nana Margarita's room was her first brush with the numinous. She remembers walking down the long hallway from the beauty shop to the kitchen, where she would get a glimpse of Nana's room. But since they weren't allowed in, she'd be filled with awe and fear. "It was truly a sacred shrine. We just can't underestimate the power of myth and ritual in our lives," Francesca says. And she frequently refers to its presence throughout her life, culminating as she works toward completing a Ph.D. in mythological studies at Pacifica Graduate Institute near Santa Barbara. A difficult marriage, a bout with alcoholism, working as a therapist of clients with eating disorders, and coming to terms with the fact that she may never have the long-desired children are some of the issues in her thirties Francesca discusses.

## A Decade of Transformation and Change

My brother, Joe, came along when I was four; when I was five, we moved to Madison, Illinois, a small town, population seven thousand, across the river. Everyone knew everyone. We owned a small business there, and the commute from St. Louis was getting to my dad; besides, we wanted to be a part of the community. It meant the five Anselmos would be leaving the large extended family to become an American nuclear family. We children spent most weekends with my grandparents, so the shock wasn't too great. And the separation and individuation was great for my mom. Madison was her territory. But I was skeptical about the move. Once again, Mom started selling: she told me about the cute house; about Kimberly, the girl next door, who was our age; and the large birthday party they had planned for Lala and me! What birthday party? I thought. My birthday was in January and my sister's was in December. This was August. It turned out that my parents had rented a hall, invited the entire kindergarten, and thrown us a "birthday party" so that we could meet our classmates. I felt guilty getting all the presents when it wasn't my birthday, but it was a great party. My parents petitioned the school board so that my sister could start school with me because they were worried we'd be sick without each other. So we were basically marketed as twins. We really don't look that much alike, but people still ask, "Are you Cheska or Lala?"

It was hard for Lala because she was a full year younger than the other kids, and she was small so the bullies picked on her. I was often in trouble coming to her rescue. Even then I relied on my wit instead of physical violence. My mother was often bailing me out of detention, which was usually due to arguing with the nun who was my teacher about some dogmatic point, most notably the role of women in the church. As I saw it, boys had a better deal: not only could they be altar boys, but they could eventually become priests, which could ultimately lead to pope, whereas girls could only be nuns, and the top of that career path was mother superior. Sister really didn't get my point, and surely she didn't enjoy debating the lack of upward mobility for women in the church, so I was banished to the hallway. Luckily, Mom was very supportive. She taught us to think, so I was always permitted to question the rules even if it meant detention. Theater, dance, and gymnastic lessons filled my extra time in grade school, and I stayed equally busy throughout high school. When I arrived at Southern Illinois University, I assumed that I'd major in theater. However, the first two shows were musicals and I couldn't sing, and that made me feel pretty disconnected. Lala and I had gone away to college together. We were even roommates, which proved to be disastrous; the sibling rivalry became too much outside the family context. On spring break, she was in a very bad motorcycle accident and dropped the rest of the semester. During her recuperation, she attended school at a different campus. For the first time in my life, I felt like I had an identity of my own. I wasn't anyone's daughter or sister. I was just me. Lala recovered, but decided to stay at her campus. That separation was probably the best thing that ever happened to us. We evolved in our separate worlds.

That summer I had to live in off-campus housing, and I just happened to live with a senior whose major was radio-TV. That fall I changed my major to radio-TV. Right away I auditioned for and received newscasts on both campus stations. I also did commercial voice-overs and wrote and acted in a children's radio program. But I didn't make TV. My roommate not only made TV, but was made news director. I was fiercely competitive at that time, and so I switched over to sales. Within a year and a half I was the sales manager.

At that time of my life, position was crucial. In my opinion there was enough time for only two out of three things: party, work, or school. I chose to work and party. I graduated with a 2.85 grade point average, but I had fifteen job offers. My college sweetheart was offered a job in Houston, and we went there over spring break for me to interview too. Just before graduation, he asked me to marry him. I considered it only because I thought my parents would have a cow if we lived together. So, with a tinge of excitement and a lot of trepidation, I came home to tell them that I was going to get married. My mom was in Chicago at the time, so I told my dad and went to bed. The next morning, my dad came into my room, sat down on the edge of my bed, touched my hand gently, and said, "Darling, we love you, and if you want to marry Andy, that's fine; we'll throw you a beautiful wedding. But we were wondering if you would consider living with him first." I gave my dad the biggest hug, and with that I went off to Houston.

After a series of unfortunate events, I decided to move home after being in Houston a little over a year. My best girlfriend was just getting out of a relationship, and we decided to live together. It took me a while to get back on my feet, but I was soon selling radio again. About nine months after I moved home, I met my future husband, Chris. We were engaged within two months, even though I had only been out of my relationship with Andy for five months. So for the second time in my life, I was living in St. Louis again.

In the mid-eighties I took some time to sell long-distance communications; being the mercurial sort that I am, I was enamored with the technology. I missed the flash of radio, though, so I eventually went back. By the late eighties, I was feeling frustrated and bored. I didn't feel that I was contributing anything to society, so I decided to go back to graduate school and get a degree in psychology. My grade point average made it nearly impossible to be accepted, but I had been a salesperson for almost ten years, and I was accepted on probation. Although I had read my share of pop psychology over the years, I had done poorly in my psychology classes in college. It's hard to do well when you don't attend class! But I loved graduate school and did very well. The last year I quit my job to go full time. I did one practicum at the community college: individual and academic counseling, registration, and coteaching assertiveness training; the other practicum at an adolescent crisis center: individual and group counseling, and casework. I was getting good grades and receiving lots of kudos. My thesis, on the epistemological differences between lucid and nonlucid dreamers, was coming along nicely. A classmate told me about a part-time family therapy position open at the Rader Institute.

Never in my wildest dreams did I think I'd work with eating disorders! It just hadn't occurred to me. I interviewed, and they hired me on the spot. I was doing multiple-family therapy and education groups. Shortly after that, I was offered what was for me a dream job. I was given another twenty hours as director of marketing, making me full time. It was a totally red-letter day. In addition to that, I had made contact with someone who was to send me the instrument I needed for my thesis.

Excitedly I rushed home from work to meet my husband and father for dinner, but Chris never showed up. The next day, he admitted that he was having an affair. I had suspected, but he had lied, saying that I was paranoid. I was devastated but relieved to know that I wasn't crazy. I threw myself into my work and was subsequently promoted rapidly through the Rader Institute. I volunteered for extra shifts and some holidays and extra projects. Then I was offered an adjunct position teaching assertiveness training at St. Louis Community College.

I worked a lot: working numbed the pain. I had always been a workaholic of sorts—America's one sanctioned addiction—and had all but abandoned my thesis. Every time I sat down at the computer, I began to cry. It was as if all that energy working and moving numbed the pain; the act of writing intensified it. Luckily I began therapy and continued to write in my journal throughout this painful process. Something angered me about a clinical issue at Rader; I resigned and went back to sell radio. My divorce was in the final stages and I was useless as a salesperson.

Finally, I reconciled with the director of Rader and I returned to part-time work. First I coordinated the partial hospitalization program, then I worked with the adolescent eating disorder patients, and then I was the sexual trauma therapist. That was a tough job. Sometimes after hearing what I heard all day, I would come home, sit down on my floor, and cry. When I finally did finish my thesis and graduate, I was offered an intake position at Rader. I saw private clients too. But when Rader offered me the position of director, I gave up the private practice. I did that for three years until the hospital canceled Rader's contract, and I did the same job for the hospital because they kept me. It was high stress, but I loved it.

In the middle of all this I applied to and enrolled at Pacifica. After my first quarter there, my boss said that it was an administrative nightmare to replace me while I was away, so I stepped down from the position and became a staff therapist. It was a drastic cut in pay, but my responsibilities were greatly diminished and my stress levels went down exponentially. Now the eating disorders program is virtually gone, but I do see eating disorders patients when they are admitted.

I went through my first existential crisis at age fourteen, which is the age I began writing in my journal. I was beginning to question my life, its purpose, and the purpose of life itself—you know, the things that existentialists ponder. I've since been through many existential crises. Many of my transformative experiences are connected with travel, and I owe part of it to the natural beauty of my destinations. There's something about the relaxed nature of a vacation that allows me to see images in a special way or notice things that I might not notice otherwise. I'm able to let in the numinous. I'm trying to emulate that consciousness on a daily basis, to allow myself to be relaxed enough to see the numinous in the images of everyday life.

When I was eight years old, my mother took us three kids on a trip out West. We traveled on a Continental Trailways bus. Those images out West—the mountains, the wide open spaces, the Native American people—transformed me. Images swirled in my head. It was an awakening of sorts. A Navajo man saved my life. Mom made us go to mass at five or six o'clock one morning; it was dark and freezing when we went into the church, and mass seemed eternal. When it was over, I ran out of the church and into the street, almost in front of an oncoming car. This very large man swooped me up and pulled me out of the way. When he put me down and I turned to thank him, he was gone. Now that was an awakening!

That experience, the beautiful images of the country, and the people have always made the West very special to me. My former husband and I made several trips out West. We went skiing every year, but the trip that really transformed me was when we spent three weeks at the Grand Canyon and the surrounding area. I had just finished watching Joseph Campbell's *The Power of Myth* series, so my mind was ripe with images of ritual and myth. We hiked to the bottom of the Grand Canyon, a grueling five-and-a-half-hour trek. As we hiked, I felt as if we were descending into the belly of the earth, climbing lower and lower into the belly of the mother. When we reached the bottom, we stayed the night at Phantom Ranch. After dinner, we went outside. It was amazing being at the bottom of this vast chasm: the sky was pitch black, myriad stars dotted the clear night sky, the shadows of small creatures danced about on the canyon walls, and as we were lying on the canyon floor looking up at this divine production, a shooting star hurled across the sky. It was clear to me that we were part of a bigger production. It was the same kind of feeling that I'd had as a child looking up at the vast expanse of space: seeing all the stars, feeling so little, but so wonderful at the same time.

When I was thirty-five, I went on a trip to Israel with my mother, and that too was an awesome experience. I was surrounded by myth and history. Jerusalem was mystical. At sunset, the limestone buildings glow. Praying at the Western Wall, I felt the presence of all who had prayed there before me; floating in the Dead Sea was whimsical; and the memorial at Yad Vashem left me speechless for an entire day. I returned home transformed. My trips to Italy have done that too. Not only have I been around my ancestral heritage in Sicily, but the art and history of Rome have sent my imagination reeling.


I quit drinking when I was thirty-six. That was another huge transformation for me. I see the world differently with sober eyes. Most of the things that I used to drink about still plague my life; I just cope with them differently. That has been the value of turning to spiritual guidance. It has been a painful journey working on myself and my soul, facing the facts I had hoped to avoid, feeling things I didn't want to feel. Now I address them head on because I no longer anesthetize myself with alcohol.

Around that time, reading *Reinventing Eve* by Kim Chernin had a profound impact on me. I read it during my labyrinthine divorce, which led me down into the underworld. I was deeply depressed, and Chernin's book helped me see my way back up from the underworld. She talks about an initiation ritual as a transition from one place to another. I did one, and it really helped. We just can't underestimate the power of myth and ritual in our lives. Then I changed my name. When I was officially divorced, I legally changed my name to Ferrentelli. My former husband had bullied me to change my name to his in the first place, and since there were no children, I decided on Ferrentelli, which was my Grandmother Sadi's name. I missed her so much, and when she died there were no more of our Ferrentellis in the United States.

My family is close, so I have that strong love bond. I know that I will always be loved. I have learned valuable lessons from both my parents. Mom always provided me with confidence. She reminded me that whatever I put my mind to, I could achieve, and she encouraged me to strive for my goals. She's pragmatic but loving and creative. When we were little and one of us came to her crying about something small like, "Joe took my coyote," she would tap-dance backward and say, "Dance with me." You had to take her hands and tap dance forward while telling her the story; she'd even call out the steps: "Buffalo Hop!" My sister hated it; I loved it. I had an audience for my woes, and it cheered me up. Dad taught me a lot about dealing with people. He's very popular, and I get that side from him. He's always been there for me—always. My brother, Joe, is shy and quiet, but when he does talk, he says the most profound things. It's that wisdom one gets from quiet introspection and silently watching the landscape. My sister lives in L.A., but we've remained very close. She's constantly leaving funny messages on my recorder, and she's listened to countless hours of existential crisis number whatever. And now, thank God, we get to see each other every month when I'm in California. My grandmother was a huge influence on me, and so was my godmother. My family is full of strong women. The common thread among these men and women is strength and humor. My sense of humor has kept me sane. It's almost a Shakespearean kind of comic relief. It does not deny the tragedy; it just makes it easier to bear.

My divorce was the best and worst thing that has ever happened to me. It was the worst because I felt pain that I didn't think I even knew how to feel. The hurt, the betrayal, the ugly things that happened when we argued over property. It was the best thing that has ever happened to me because it launched me into a journey of transformation and self-discovery—a journey that would have taken longer or maybe never have even happened without it.

I had read in Sophia Loren's autobiography when I was nineteen that she told some producer off when he suggested she lose weight and get a nose job. I thought, "What self-confidence!" I wanted to have that level of self-confidence to be able to say, "This is me, take it or leave it!"

Due to the pain and shock of separation, I got into therapy. Realizing that I had other issues, I stayed for a while. I learned to stand up for myself and my convictions. I was always assertive, but I learned to be more so. I learned to know what I want and to ask for it, and I've learned to express myself better.

Chris and I went to marital therapy, but I was uncertain as to whether our marriage had a chance. Then at our final session he said, "This marriage can't handle a baby or a Ph.D." I had been lobbying for a baby, and I also knew I wanted to continue my education. I knew that it was over, that I couldn't give away everything I wanted just to stay in that relationship. I had worked too hard to learn who I was and to determine what I wanted to throw it all away. I still don't have children, and that continues to be a big wound for me, but I am working on my doctorate. There, I am birthing something in my studies at Pacifica. It may not be a literal baby, but it is new life nonetheless. As a result of the divorce, I'm stronger, more vulnerable, more cynical, more optimistic. And I'm funnier.

Early menopause runs in my family and I was fearful, despite that my gynecologist had ruled out any sign of perimenopause. I had been in a tentative and unpredictable relationship, but when he moved from the Pacific Northwest and accepted a job in St. Louis to be with me, I felt a little safer. My little inner voice said, "Run screaming!" but I loved him, retained hope, and agreed to stay in the relationship. When I told him that I wanted to get married and have children, he told me he wasn't ready for that level of commitment—he didn't know if he would ever be ready. I was devastated, just devastated. We broke up, and I began drinking heavily, mostly in private, which further intensified my angst. Then I developed an ulcer. There I was, thirty-five years old, educated, a professional, single, childless; drinking Maalox by the refrigerator light; and I said to myself "You're a statistic!"

When I was thirty-six, I began having hot flashes, night sweats, and insomnia; I panicked. It turned out to be a hormonal imbalance that was easily treated, but my distress increased exponentially. Meanwhile I was not in a relationship. When I got sober, I made the commitment to stay out of a relationship for a year. It was hard because I was very conscious of my age, and I still wanted a chance to get married and have a child. I could almost hear my clock ticking away. But I needed to stay sober, and I was completely aware that so much of my drinking had been about love gone awry. I spent countless hours crying, grieving, hoping, praying. My anxiety was exacerbated by the fact that I'd had an abortion in my early twenties. Even though I'm prochoice and wouldn't have done anything different, the old grief flooded back. It was still a loss. A loss is a loss—whether it's an abortion, a miscarriage, or giving a child up for adoption—and it needs to be grieved. Luckily Sicilians know how to do grief in a big way. Who knows how things will turn out, but I am painfully aware that there are hundreds of thousands of women who feel similar things.

My greatest sorrow is that I don't have a relationship and that I haven't had or don't have children. That has been a hard one. It's a hard one for a lot of women. But I realize that I have made choices. I have made choices in relationships and in my career that have contributed to that outcome. But I still feel sad. Being childless is a great loss for me. And the older I get, the further it feels from my reach. I realize there are lots of options for women; I just wanted them in the context of a committed relationship. The relationship I had been in ended recently, and with school and working full time, I'm just too busy to meet someone new. It's not that I need a man to feel complete; I have been without a partner most of my thirties. I just want a romantic relationship, to have Aphrodite and Eros in my life.

I want to tell other women to pursue their passions, to trust themselves and their instincts, to do what they want—not what they think they're supposed to do. We have choices; we can virtually do whatever we want. But our choices do have consequences. I think we were sold a bill of goods when we were told that women could do it all: marriage, career, children, social life. A lot of women are very stressed trying to balance all of that. Believe me, I have been a therapist long enough to know the issues women present. It's not true: we can't do it all, not without consequences. If we try, we run the risk of doing some things badly, or doing them devoid of soul, or we may exhaust ourselves trying to keep all the balls in the air. Granted, there are some extraordinary women who are able to pull it off, but on the whole it's just savvy marketing. It's putting a feminine ideal into a masculine role. The media are constantly telling us what we want and how we feel. My advice to someone else is this: Take time; figure out what *you* want—the thing that makes *you* happy. Then allow yourself to do it. You can't get what you want unless you know what you want, and then you can devise a plan to get it.

Right now my life is dominated by work and school, but I do take time off to spend time with my friends or family. I'm very domestic. My house is orderly, and I love to come home and chill out and look at my art or take a catnap. I've always eaten in a healthy manner, and being an eating disorder therapist has increased my proclivity to do so. And I love to cook. Most of my cooking is done while I'm on my cordless phone returning calls. Astonished friends will say, "When did you have the time to make this?" and I'll say, "Last night when I was talking to you on the phone." I bake a lot, and I make a mean lasagna. On Monday nights I host a half-hour talk radio program called "Psych Talk." I interview health care professionals on psychological and related issues. I love doing the show, and I've had some interesting guests.

Romance is the area of my life that has been strangely lacking. I'd been seeing someone for a year when we saw that our spiritual and philosophical differences couldn't be overcome, and we decided to break up. I was very sad. Not only was I grieving the loss of the relationship, but I had just turned thirty-nine, and I felt that my biological clock was ticking faster than a New York taxi meter. So in actuality I was grieving two things: him and the hope of a baby. The spare time I do have I spend with friends and family because that feeds me; those visits energize me. With school I feel that I have been too busy to take the time to meet someone. But it goes back to what I said about choices. I'm aware that I have made the choice to pursue a doctorate, and that's a huge investment of time and energy. I have to trust in the universe.

When I am old, I plan to be healthy and spunky; that's part of why I live a healthy lifestyle now. I don't plan any plastic surgery; I want to age naturally. So much of my work in eating disorders focuses on self-esteem, and I want to love myself the way I am, not how society thinks I should be. I want to hang out with my friends and family laughing about our history and making new history. I want to look back at my old journals and reflect on my musings, and I want to continue musing. And by then maybe I'll have learned to whistle.

The most important lesson I have learned is to trust my instincts, to listen to that tiny inner voice—which now is not so tiny—that warns me or encourages me; it's almost always right. Meditation has given her a louder voice, and so now she's easier to hear. There have been times that I have ignored her, which is evident to me in my journal writing. There are numerous occasions when I'd begun to address a problem or issue; then conveniently there are no entries for a month—just long enough for me to deny the issue and sometimes even act in defiance of the insight.

Success comes in many forms: financial, professional, personal, artistic. I'm most concerned with being a success as a person. For me that comes in relating to my friends, family, and community. I have been very successful in that way. One thing that I am very proud of is that most of my friends have been in my life for a very long time. I have worked to cultivate, honor, and nurture them. There is something very comforting about having friends for twenty and twenty-five years. Even my "new" friends have been around for years.

My best friend, Ellen, and I have been friends since I was sixteen and she was fourteen. There have been times when we haven't seen each other for a while, and when we do, we have the same glasses. It's got to be a metaphor that we still see the world in the same way. We've been through a lot together.

Doing what you love and loving what you do is another hallmark of success for me. Thank God, I love what I do! I feel very blessed.

I was very excited about my thirtieth birthday! I was still married and my former husband took me to Tony's (then St. Louis's only five-star restaurant) and presented me with diamond earrings. We had a very romantic, wonderful time. We took my car; I was driving a Porsche 944 at the time. I felt I'd arrived. Boy, how things can change. My dad gave me a bottle of expensive champagne, flowers, and balloons. My brother gave me a concrete deer for the garden with a red bow around its neck. They had the whole house decorated. My sister called from California, and my mom lavished me with clothes. I was so happy—not because of the material things but for the sense of connectedness. I remember thinking to myself, "I'm married to a man I'm crazy about, I'm in graduate school and I love it, and when I get out, we're going to have a baby!" Little did I know I would be navigating a vastly different landscape within eighteen months.

My last birthday was thirty-nine. I had just broken up with my boyfriend, I was grieving the baby issue, and to make matters worse I was sick. A nasty flulike virus had spread around, and I was down for the count. I had already been in bed for a day and a half, and my voice was gone. My radio show would be on in three days, so I knew I needed to conserve my voice. To thicken the plot, St. Louis was under about a foot of snow and ice. On some streets, the snowplows had come by, and the snow was blocking in cars with a three- to four-foot wall of frozen snow.

Everyone called to see how I was doing. Ellen and her husband, John, paid three neighborhood boys handsomely to dig out their car. Then John drove the six blocks to me; we stopped by the store on the way to their house and later feasted on steak and lobster. Earlier that morning I had been lamenting my woeful lot, and by evening I was grateful that I have people who love me so much.

My thirties have been a decade of transformation and change. In some ways it has been my most painful decade; in some ways it has been my best so far. One thing is certain: it has been a time when I've allowed myself to flourish. I figured out what I wanted, and I either took steps to get it or I asked for it. I learned a lot from age thirty to now. My birthday is January 2, so I virtually have a calendar year from birthday to birthday, and each year I reflect on what has happened.

My early thirties were easy! I was married (happily, I thought) to a man I loved, in graduate school and loving it, about to make a career change. Then there was the separation and divorce and rebuilding my life, which has been a long, painful, and rewarding process. My confidence level has soared. I saw that I was able to do things on my own. Things that some people took for granted gave me tremendous pride and satisfaction. I had my own ladder and tools, and I hung all my own paintings; I fixed things, and I made my own decisions; things were taking off professionally. I was having fun. It wasn't until I was thirty-five that I began to feel angst over getting married and having children. At thirty-six I got sober, and by the end of my thirty-seventh year, I was back in school. Now in my thirty-ninth year, I can look forward to another decade. Most of the women I know have experienced similar growth and transformation in their thirties. I guess we benefit by applying what we have learned the first twenty-nine years.

I have learned to love my body, and it's a love that is hard won. Although my own body image issues have helped me to understand women with eating disorders, they have caused me undue pressure and pain. In the past, when someone made a negative comment about my body, I always felt terrible, whether it was an innocent comment or a malicious attack—and both have happened plenty. I have experienced internal and external pressure to be thinner; both rage tyranny on our souls. How can we truly love ourselves if we love ourselves on a contingency basis: "I'll feel better about myself; I'll like myself more if I can just lose weight." That kind of thinking is lethal. We are plagued with a media-imposed image of beauty, an image that only 1 percent of women even have the genetic predisposition to achieve. Yet we have a whole culture striving to acquire it.

Today my attitude is a bit like Sophia Loren: this is it; this is how I am; take it or leave it. It amazes me how a dress size or a number on the scale has the power to dictate how a woman feels about herself! How is it that we can let this seemingly unrelated entity measure our self-worth? But we do, and we do it in droves. First we need to derive our self-worth from inside. We need to remember that bodies come in all shapes and sizes. We need to educate our children as early as possible to feel good about themselves and about their bodies. Americans unknowingly vote with their dollars: what we buy comes back for another term in office, so to speak. Because we are obsessed with thinness as a culture; new products arrive on the shelves at a dizzying pace. We need to stamp our feet and just say no to the multibillion dollar per year diet industry. We need to elect it out of office. What happened to that full-breasted, full-hipped look? If we deny her, we deny an important aspect of the feminine.

*My advice to other women who have visions or passions and want to pursue them is: by all means, pursue them, pursue them, pursue them, with eyes wide open as to the sacrifices necessary to live your vision and the incalculable rewards. We all have our particular gift to share with this world. If we ignore our gift, through insecurities, or fear, or even laziness, we cheat the world of hearing our voice and knowing our unique process.*

MONICA PRABA PILAR

# Monica Praba Pilar

## PROFILE

According to artist Monica Praba Pilar, "Politicians don't do art; artists can't do politics." But the arts and political activism are her all-consuming passions. In 1979, at age fifteen, she volunteered to work for the Jimmy Carter presidential campaign because she was terrified at the prospect of having Ronald Reagan as president. Of course, Reagan was elected, and her destiny as a political activist was set. At age seventeen she entered New York University to study political science and work to stop the U.S. military intervention in Central America. At age twenty, she left to join the ray of hope in the political madness of the era, a chance to engage in the politics of meaning in Jesse Jackson's Rainbow Coalition presidential campaign.

As Monica says, "Who wanted to be in academia when there was a chance to actually stop the American intervention in Central America? Not I." She worked for Jesse Jackson, then moved on to work on the campaigns of Congressman Ed Towns (Democrat) and Congressman Major Owens (Democrat), in her home town, Brooklyn, New York.

In a paraphrase from Ludwig Wittgenstein's *Tractatus Logico-Philosophicus,* Monica believes that "environment affects life, life imitates art, art therefore must be life." She gives veracity to this point of view by engaging in projects that evolve out of political, social, or personal events. Joan Kiley, the executive director of Community Recovery Services, a Berkeley nonprofit organization for alcoholic recovery, says of her, "Praba is continually developing projects that reflect her community involvement, her vision of art as an integral part of community, as well as her own growth and healing process." Monica explores approaches to alternative methods of communication through performance, installations, sculpture, audio, video, or "whatever means necessary that have yet to be invented."

As a Latina with Argentinian, Colombian, and American roots, she asks, "And what does being Latina have to do with any of this? Everything. Where would I be without Celia Cruz and Willie Colon? Without Mercedes Sosa and Suzanna Baca? In an asylum for the politically aware? *Quien sabe?* But thanks to my roots in Colombian culture, I still know how to enjoy life."

## Pursuing a Vision

I was born in a taxi in New York City on the way to the hospital, small and feisty and ready to take on the world. More than anything else as a child, I wanted to be with my sister, who was five years older, and my brother, who was only a year and a half older. When I was two, I demanded to be let into school with them to learn everything they knew, and I was always in a continuous state of catch up and run and catch up. I had boundless energy and curiosity about the world.

We moved often when I was a child because of my father's work. When I was five months old, we moved from New York City to Argentina, where my father is from; later to Colombia, where my mother is from; and subsequently to Venezuela, Mexico, Texas, and other places, and finally back to

New York City. Always migrating, I developed an early sense of being an outsider, of being resilient and self-reliant. I learned to expect surprises and not to depend on the foreseen.

My mother is strong and independent and a real survivor. She has a strong sense of fun and a capacity for unconditional love that I've rarely seen in life. She taught me to read when I was three and filled my life with literature, art, travel, adventure, and love. Although she often worked full time and was sometimes the sole supporter of our family, she always strived to give us a sense of family unity. An early feminist, she encouraged me to set the highest goals and supported my sister and me in imagining a life beyond any culturally prescribed female roles.

Happiness is a habit I learned from my mom. Her joie de vivre is contagious, and my brother and I were lucky to get a full dose. I've had many joys in my life: being an artist; having been present for my incredible sister; being open to the kindness of people; what I've learned from the men I've loved, the women I've shared with, and the ultimate unfolding gifts of creativity that surround us.

My father, on the other hand, was a salesman who fortunately disappeared on extended business trips. He had severe untreated psychological problems, which marred our entire family and had a destructive effect on all of us. He never resolved these problems and died an isolated and bitter man. He inadvertently taught me a lot about oppression.

We went through a lot of upheavals and very difficult times with accidents, illnesses, disasters, and calamities, which had a very disorienting effect on me. My father was continuously ill with multiple heart attacks and surgeries and repeatedly in and out of the hospital. My brother almost died when I was ten. My mom disappeared for a short period when I was eleven; at the time, I imagined she'd never come back. My grandmother went into a coma while I was visiting her when I was twelve, and she died shortly after. My sister became ill with an undiagnosable illness. And on it went. The irrationality and totalitarianism of my father deepened my growing sense of dread and doom.

Simultaneously, our migrations through different cultures and areas were revealing the ugly brutality of the world. When we moved to Texas, I was exposed to the full brunt of the learned racism of children. We lived in a small border town where Mexicans and Anglos did not mix well. We moved into an Anglo neighborhood, and everyone assumed we were Mexican. I was often subjected to scapegoating and separated out in school for being the "other."

I came into adolescence with a great deal of anger and engaged in a deep and sustained rebellion against the lessons of my father, which took many years to resolve. Ultimately, this led me to work against oppression and injustice in the broader context. They are elements I understand all too closely.

I cut my teeth on the Jimmy Carter presidential campaign when I was fifteen, out of opposition to Ronald Reagan. I was an early and full-bloomed progressive, and my goals then were to work for the United Nations, challenging development policy and institutionalizing the alternative development ideas of E. F. Schumacher. I went to New York University when I was seventeen to study anthropology, economics, and development theory. Corruption entirely paralyzed the international development process, as it does today. The field was riddled with disastrous and ecologically destructive short-term projects with very short-term profits only for the politicians involved.

I became much more interested in community organizing and in direct action campaigns. The time I was at NYU was a wonderful period to meet other radicals and work together on direct action campaigns, from South Africa solidarity to housing in New York City, to opposing U.S. intervention in Central America under Reagan. I left college to work for the Jesse Jackson Rainbow Coalition presidential campaign. I felt he brought together a multiracial, multicultural, progressive platform.

As the years passed I grew frustrated with the limits of political work and turned to the visual arts. I enrolled in a unique school in New York City, the Arts Students League, where no one pushed us to see art as a marketable commodity. "Art for art's sake" was the motto; money and sales of one's work were never discussed. Over the next seven or eight years, I studied art at three other schools, ending up on the West Coast at the San Francisco Art Institute. While I was there, I began to explore three-dimensional work and create site installations.

As an artist I try to invent projects where I can integrate political work and community work with art. I'm equally moved by personal stories about loss, the unconscious, and the spiritual roots of all life.

My advice to other women who have visions or passions and want to pursue them is: Pursue them, pursue them, pursue them, by all means, with eyes wide open as to the sacrifices necessary to live your vision and the incalculable rewards. We all have our particular gift to share with this world. If we ignore our gift, through insecurities, or fear, or even laziness, we cheat the world of hearing our voice and knowing our unique process. I've lived through challenging periods in order to live my vision as an artist, and I wouldn't change a single thing.

The stronger your values and commitment, the easier the road.


My brother has been the most meaningful point of transformation for me. Being only eighteen months older, he was my closest ally and double and source of mischief and all kinds of trouble and fun. He cracked his skull in an accident when I was ten and went into a coma, floating unconscious between life and death for two weeks, calling out my name. The sight of him unconscious in the hospital with a bandage around his head filled me with the worst fear and dread and anguish. Eventually he recovered and came back home. He introduced me to Plato's Dialogues when I was thirteen, to Alan Watts, to Karen Horney, and he always demanded that, as Rilke wrote, I "live the questions themselves." We share a deep love of poetry, literature, music, art, and radical politics, but it is his deep spirituality and sharing of innate knowledge, combined with his unswerving commitment to challenging me to confront pain and overcome it, that has been the most transformative element of my life. To love the questions themselves, to transcend the brutality that wounds you, to open to life as the creative force. I don't think I'd be alive now if my brother had not repeatedly reached deep into my soul, shaken me up, and broken through. I feel grateful every day to have him in my life.

A curator named Inverna Lockpez ran INTAR Gallery in the 1980s, show-ing the work of contemporary Latin American and U.S.-born Latina and Latino artists. I worked for her for a year or two in my early twenties. She was an indomitable Latin American woman with a tremendous sense of humor and a wonderfully developed sense of the absurd, balanced by a sim-ple and genuine humanism. It amused me how intimidated men were by her power and the games they would try to play to negate that. I learned a lot from her response: she never played along; she was far too self-directed and independent to waste her time. She was a visionary, a feminist, a hu-manist, and an artist, and she imprinted on me the sheer force of power a woman can and should have in the world.

Another role model was Louise Roberts, a dancer who ran her own dance company in New York City. I met her when I was in my early twen-ties and she was in her seventies, and we became great friends. She was an incredibly generous artist, sharing her love of life, her knowledge, her love, her feistiness, her independence, her depth, her spirit. Although living on the margin herself, she personally supported many dancers who in the 1980s were getting very sick with AIDS. She moved a number of young dancers into her apartment and cared for them while supporting them financially; their own families denied what was happening or abandoned them. Louise was fearless, adventurous, independent, intelligent, very much fun, and eth-ical, and she always imparted her sense of our shared responsibility for each other. The depth of love I feel for Louise is primordial and ultimately re-flects the gratitude I feel for the plenitude of gifts she has shared with me as a friend and mentor. Hers were all gifts of the most basic and just human-ity, never to be lost or squandered.

A woman I endlessly admire and who has had a very powerful influ-ence on me is the bioenergetics therapist Naomi O'Keefe, from San Fran-cisco. Her interest in violence and in the transformation of hate in people led her to long and complex philosophical and spiritual studies and ulti-mately into bioenergetics. The work I did with her over four years was in-credibly difficult and challenging; she shared her experience of authenticity and of the ability of all people to be transformed into creative forces. She is the most beautiful, life-affirming, and authentic womanist I know.

Nelson Mandela is living testament to the ability of ordinary human beings to challenge destructive and inhuman strictures dictatorially imposed by those in power and to prevail, even through great personal sacrifice.

Apartheid was an absolutely intolerable system of governance. The anti-apartheid movement in and beyond South Africa taught me that we can and must work to challenge injustice, even when the cost may be our own life.

Racism in all of its insidious manifestations drives me insane. I think it is the root of evil—the most destructive force on earth and the cause of very real suffering for the majority of humanity. A cursory study of the Third Reich, apartheid, the eugenics movement, multiple genocides, and all the other brutality suffered through wars around the world will always reveal racism as the root cause.

My greatest sorrow is the harsh illness and unexpected death of my sister, Sandra, when she was thirty-five. She had a disabling gastrointestinal illness (Chrohn's disease) and was devastatingly ill for over seventeen years. She dealt with her illness with amazing equanimity, through many operations, repeated hospitalizations, invasive treatments, dizzying drugs, constant disability, and worse. My mom, brother, and I never left her alone and tried to share her burden as much as anyone can. Just as she came to terms with herself, her illness, her life, her God, she died, alone in a hospital in New York. I had been her primary caretaker for years, and the anguish caused by her death was unspeakable. The sorrow has made me confront very painful spiritual lessons of life, death, and the incomprehensible suffering implied.

I've seen so much physical suffering and so many people I've loved have died. It is difficult for me even to talk about it. This is the most important lesson for me. I've seen inexplicable suffering, illness, tragedy in friends, family, loved ones and beyond; difficult and painful deaths; lives cut off senselessly; people abandoned in hospitals and in death. I can't understand it, let go of it, accept it. In that moment, where is faith? Where is meaning? Where is justice? Where is life? I've had to search deeply within my soul for an acceptance of suffering and death, an acceptance full with life, with creativity, with joy, without anger and bitterness, and still continue to search for that presence that meets life without holding back for all that pain.

I spend as much time with family and friends as humanly possible. Friends and family are so enriching! I often end up somehow or other working with friends, which is great, because it gives us time to see each other and share our creative process. My best friend, however, is someone I've never worked with, is not an artist, and does not even live near me anymore. She is simply someone whom I feel deliriously happy around, and I try to see her or talk with her as much as I can, although she never really leaves my mind.

I hardly have any free time; between art work, political activism, community commitments, and financial commitments, I would say I can give only about 15 percent of my time to my romantic endeavors, which no man appreciates! I find myself in a quandary: demanding complete, unequivocal, and absolute independence while craving a man on call, hopefully waiting by the phone for my call. Awful.

My mom has been an amazing role model for aging. She never believed any of the stereotypes about women and has moved through her life fearlessly! I have watched her move through her fifties and sixties, and into her seventies, with the same sense of adventure, the same joie de vivre, the same confidence, and the same ability to know what she wants and just do it. My fantasy of aging is that I will know more and care less, and will be as irreverent in the face of predictable elderly elegance as she is.

The most smashing success of all is the ability to live life with integrity and authenticity! This cannot ever be stolen, taken away, lost, or destroyed; it carries within and throughout life. I want to be part of a worldwide cultural renaissance and movement toward a just and sustainable world. I'm holding out for that.

I was deathly ill the entire year before my thirtieth birthday and wasn't sure I'd even make it. Disabled by illness, trapped at home, I spent my time frustrated and angry over my illness, my inability to meet my goals, mulling over every mistake I'd ever made. It was a year of self-recriminations: "You didn't do this by your thirties; you didn't do that! What kind of woman are you!" I feared for my sanity and thought the actual birthday would be ruinous. The actual birthday was surprisingly anticlimactic. I immediately let go of all that crap on that day. The mixture of thinking I could die with the expectations to "have it altogether and worked out by your thirties" was a very bad one. I hardly even note birthdays any more and certainly do not think about aging in preordained time capsules with arbitrary rules.

All the women I know have been able to enjoy much more self-acceptance and confidence in their thirties. For me, it has represented a period where I can actualize many of my dreams, as the things I did in my twenties come together in increasingly more meaningful ways. In retrospect, it's as if in my twenties I was gathering information about the world and my role in it, and in my thirties I've been able to put some of that information to work within the larger society.

I cannot believe the vapidness of Western culture in the late 1990s! The encouragement to alter one's body surgically to meet an arbitrary standard has increased exponentially. Are any of these people really happier? All of the women I know have become more beautiful as they unsurgically age, precisely because of interior changes in outlook that have led them to be more self-accepting.

Women cannot afford to believe the hype put on them by corporate advertising and consumerist culture. Mores are changing constantly and are so arbitrary! I make an effort to avoid corporate advertising and deal with all the b.s. by reading more poetry. A couple of hours with Alice Walker's "Revolutionary Petunias," or with Julia de Burgos's "For You, Julia de Burgos" cures any of my self-image blues.

The issue of children is very tricky terrain. I'm coming close to having the decision made for me physically and am still undecided! I find it hard to imagine creating a new life, with all the love, hope, nurturing, and joy, and then letting it go into this brutal, unpredictable world. Then there is the consideration of how a full-time artist enacts good motherhood. Beats me! I don't see many examples of happy women artist mothers. Something usually has to give.

I was lucky enough to be taken to India by my brother, who dragged my mom and me along. Two different years we went to the ashram of Osho and spent months meditating. This has been the most meaningful personal experience of my life; I was rechristened as Praba, meaning, "life radiance." The meditations helped me get beyond my own seriousness and develop a sense of humor about the brutality of human stupidity. I'm always trying to combine artmaking with meditating, being more aware as I spend hours and hours and hours in silence and solitude on an art process. Creative expression is the absolute vastness of all and everything to me, from the subatomic level to the transgalactic. It is the origin and the unfolding.

In my next decade I'd love to see a cultural renaissance where artists are the visionaries, where we challenge the forces that are bringing us to the brink of biodevastation and ecocide. My goal is to inspire as many people as possible to understand that ordinary people have extraordinary impact on the world, precisely because we all collectively carry responsibility for the institutions we've created to live under.

*It was in my thirties that I began to be able to choose what I wanted to do and go toward that. I don't think you can do that in your twenties, no matter where you come from, because you're dealing with so much; you don't have the experience and you're carrying baggage from your childhood. It's so chaotic in the twenties. It's not until your thirties that you actually have a choice.*

IKAZO

# Ikazo

## PROFILE

When I first met Ikazo in 1988, we were both participants in Deena Metzger's women's writing group held on Wednesday evenings at her home in Topanga, a rustic canyon thirty minutes north of Los Angeles. Ikazo never spoke to the group, unless it was to read her writing from the previous week or what she had just written in that evening's class. To say that she seemed like a wounded, frightened bird is not hyperbole. It wasn't just the blue jay feathers and beads she wore in her hair or her unkempt appearance. There was a wildness about Ikazo that could have belonged to a preying red-tailed hawk; yet a sweetness too, like that found in the heart-shaped face of a barn owl. Unmistakably, here was a punctured soul with a lacerated sense of self. Her guilelessness enchanted us all. That's why it was so monstrous to hear writing that was filled with such violent, even lurid details of an atrocious childhood, yet so splendidly, even poetically, written. Ikazo has the gift: the gift of good writing.

I laughed with delight when I told Ikazo that I had always wanted to include her in one of my books, and now I finally had the opportunity. She laughed too, in her abandoned way that has replaced the guarded,

**97**

protective stance she used to bear. A fresh life has emerged from the injured shell I first knew, and Ikazo would be the first to credit Deena Metzger who taught her (and has taught so many others, including myself) to write for her life. That writing has now become a novel, *Out of the Forest of Nowards.* Here Ikazo discusses her novel, living on the earth in Topanga, her childhood, and how writing saved her life.

# Making Choices

I'm writing a novel now, about a young Japanese American woman who confronts her own madness after having spent her entire adult life as a prostitute and drug addict. When she turns to her childhood, she sees where the seeds of prostitution were planted in her by her own parents. It deals with patriarchal archetypes of culture. So some of the seeds are cultural and come from Japan's male-dominated society. In tracing her history, she goes back to her grandparents on either side and discovers certain realities inherent within their cultural background. But there is also the immigrant experience, and the deep psychological wounds that the American concentration camps inflicted on Japanese immigrants and their American-born children when they were condemned behind barbed wire after being incarcerated in 1942 through 1944. Both her parents endured incarceration along with the grandparents who were still living at that time.

My grandmother was a picture bride. My grandfather immigrated to America when he was seventeen. Soon after his twenty-third birthday, while he was working as a cook and butler for a Caucasian family, he decided to get married. He picked my grandmother, Komatsu, through an exchange of photographs, common practice among Japanese men living in the United States who were interested in marriage.

At one time prostitution in Japan was considered legal, and it was common practice for a poor family to send their daughter to a house of prostitution so that she could help support the family. Only after the introduction of the West and Western ideas was this practice frowned on and considered wrong. After the war, attitudes had changed, and many prostitutes returned home to find that instead of being celebrated, they had been disowned by the very families who sent them to places such as Burma, where houses of prostitution flourished. *Sandakan Brothel Number 8* by Yamazaki Tomoko illustrates the life of one of these women.

Look at the story of the Korean women, known as "comfort women," who were sold into prostitution in the Japanese "recreation camps" of World War II, which we are just finding out about. Nora Okja Keller writes about this in *Comfort Women*.

Japanese women are trained to be submissive. There used to be a saying that a Japanese woman followed two steps behind her husband, usually carrying his luggage. Today, in the larger cities in Japan, some things are changing. Women have become more aggressive, but it is still mostly men, I think, who run the big businesses.

When people ask me what I do, I generally say that I'm an artist. For the past ten years, I've made my living as a landscape designer. Creating a landscape is like painting, only instead of using paints I'm using plants and flowers for color. And the canvas is huge. That's the part I like.

I started painting very early. I began to use oils at the age of twelve, and drawing, I've always drawn since I was a toddler. By the time I was seventeen, I was pretty much of a figurative painter and photorealist. I was also doing commissioned work as a portrait painter. I was never an abstract painter. I love the human body for what it is. My own paintings always had a certain darkness to them.

I had a very dark childhood, which led to a very disturbing adulthood. But this darkness also brought my creativity into existence. I think my imagination kept me alive.

I've had a very hard life. I never imagined my life to be so difficult. Then again, I've had an extraordinarily varied and interesting life. At the age of twelve I decided I needed to take my life in my own hands, so I ran away from Chicago, where I had been raised, to Los Angeles. I faked a school ID and bought a plane ticket over the phone. For a while I was a juvenile delinquent. Since that time I've seen and dealt with quite a lot.

At about that time I met a man who was much older than I was. I was twenty, twenty-one, and very naive. I had been disowned from my family and I lived with this man who became very abusive to me. I became afraid to leave because he said he would find me and break my legs and mess up my face. At twenty-one I believed him. Now of course I would inform the police. I would leave at once. I would encourage anyone in a physically abuse relationship to get out and get help. At one point he forced me to burn all my drawings, and one day I came home to find five of my paintings disfigured. He had written across the face of them, "What about me?" in large white letters. I stopped painting then.

I was getting no information from my parents on how to live a life. Some of this, I believe now, was caused by their incarceration at the time in their lives when they should have been preparing for adulthood. My father had been preparing to go to college. He was salutatorian of his high school class. The war and the camps came along and wiped out his future.

When I hit my thirties, I decided to go after the truth, no matter how painful. That was a hard thing to do, having been raised in a Japanese American family where silence is the name of the game. I'd been living in the dark until then. Now I began what some people call the spiritual quest. I began looking for a much deeper meaning to my life. My twenties had been chaotic, and suddenly I was hitting thirty. I left my life as it was in Chicago and came out to California. I was headed for Esalen Institute, in Big Sur. I was having a nervous breakdown. I was psychotic, and I didn't want to be hospitalized and treated with traditional medications, which had happened to me before.

I thought that psychosis was something inside me that needed to come out. I packed up my three-bedroom apartment in Chicago and put everything into storage. Esalen Institute was booked up full, and it wasn't until I got to Wyoming that I found out there was one spot open for me. Someone had canceled. So I went to Esalen to have what they called a spiritual breakthrough.

My last birthday was spectacular. I gathered my closest friends, my new lover, and my longtime lover from Chicago, Katherine, and a number of other very close friends and we all sat in a circle in the high wheat and talked about how much we all loved each other! It was quite an incredible experience. It lasted all afternoon; there was much laughter and love, and we followed the arc of the sun.

By late afternoon one could see the circles we had made in the high wheat because the wheat was pressed down. It reminded me of what community was like in one of Jean Giono's early novels, *The Joy of Man's Desiring* or *Song of the World*.

There's still a lot I haven't done in my life that I wish to do. I want to finish writing the manuscript I'm writing now, and then I want to start on my second novel, which will be about a family that is split between being incarcerated in the American internment camps and Japan. I also want to go to Japan and visit the Hiroshima Memorial. I don't think America has ever really seriously looked at what it did when it dropped the bomb.

The effects of the American concentration camps have not been acknowledged much because so many North American Japanese are quiet about that particular experience. Even after they were interned, they never talked about it, if ever, for years. Their children never knew. My parents never told me. Most of the other kids who were sansei (third-generation Japanese in America) had no idea either. Among other things, I think it instilled in the nisei (the second-generation Japanese Americans—my parents) a sense of shame and of having to deny the whole experience in order to keep face, which is a cultural expectation. So we kids grew up with this sense of being stigmatized; there was something we should be ashamed of, but we didn't know what it was about, since our parents kept quiet about the camps. One grew up trying to please, to be accepted, to fit in with the norm, and a part of this—girls growing up trying to please—is also part of the Japanese culture.

My life has been so different from that of other Japanese American women, because I rebelled against my family and went delinquent. You didn't find many delinquent Japanese American kids during the sixties and seventies. I thought that was rebellion, but ultimately it's the reverse.

My novel is also about incest, which in a way is also a part of my background. But I completely denied this as a teenager and young adult. Entering young adulthood, I had no tools to go out into the world with. So when I came into my young adult life, I was picked up by a really destructive and evil character. In the novel, the young girl is picked up by a pimp, who gets her involved with prostitution. The girl is taken to Europe, where she is put out on the streets in Milan. She doesn't even speak the language. She's so naive she doesn't even know that she could call the American embassy to get back to America. After a few years, she works her way up to becoming a high-class call girl making lots of money. She finally sees an Asian client, a Chinese man, who comes over to her apartment and they have sex. As he is turning around to dress himself, she recognizes her own father's back. Thus begins her journey out of that kind of life.

At a certain point I moved in with the woman who had invited me to Esalen. She lived in a rural canyon in Los Angeles. But because I was still going through the experience of breaking down, it was very difficult for her, and I was taken in by a writer and healing teacher named Deena Metzger.

Deena offered me a camper trailer that had previously belonged to an artist named Vijli. And so I moved to Deena's. I didn't really move into that camper trailer, though. I sort of lived outside for a year, and Deena just basically left me alone and let me do whatever it was I needed to do. I needed to sort through things, I guess, and it took all my attention and energy. It was very painful. I was like an animal because I didn't have the energy to attend to myself.

So that was the beginning of my thirties. And after that I did reintegrate at some point, and I reentered society and I started a landscaping business. I have a very good business now. I never dreamed of becoming a landscaper, but I love the work. So it was in my thirties that I began to be able to choose what I wanted to do and go toward that. I don't think you can do that in your twenties, no matter where you come from, because you're dealing with so much, and it's so chaotic. You don't have the experience, and some of us are carrying baggage from our childhood. It's not until your thirties that you actually have a choice. Then in your forties, I think, everything probably sort of begins melding together, and even more choices may become available to you.

After the 1960s, there was a dynamic change in the way in which women began relating to sex. I was born into an era that guaranteed me the right to have an orgasm and to enjoy that orgasm. My mother certainly wasn't born into any such era. A part of it was the women's movement, but a larger part, I believe, was the breakdown of secularism in religion, the weakening role of the church, the onslaught of psychology, and the introduction of the birth control pill.

I think once women realized that they could enjoy sex as much as men—and that came from the mere fact that there was no longer the fear of getting pregnant if they didn't want to get pregnant—it changed them. Women were released from getting pregnant, so suddenly they could enjoy sex, and I think that made a lot of difference for women being able to go after what they wanted. That kind of sexual equality made women much more powerful. In other cultures, especially indigenous cultures, women are still tied down to having babies and caring for babies, and if it is a religious culture, then certainly the women are still completely dominated by men.

The advice I would give someone younger than myself would depend on what her issues were. I'm thinking about this young seventeen-year-old who really is a very good writer, if she had a chance. That chance would have to come through outside influence. She doesn't have a chance in her own world. She would have to be introduced to those opportunities—such things as scholarships and education.

I didn't come from a family where girls were sent to college. The boys were expected to go and were sent to college. My father said to me, "You're a girl so you don't have to earn a living; you can get married. But the boys have to support a family so they need to go to college." I was so pissed off about that that I robbed a bank to go to college. That's how I got into the

University of Illinois, but then I got a scholarship. A black teacher took me under his wing. Last year, I decided to get my M.F.A. in writing, so I enrolled at Goddard College in Vermont.

In ancient Japan, around the sixteenth century, prostitutes were considered shamans; they were exempt from society's rules and were looked up to in many ways. This is different from the geishas in Arthur Golden's best-selling book, *Memoirs of a Geisha*. It's well written and he must have done a lot of research, but I believe he totally romanticized the geisha. Prostitution is not romantic. The woman he said he interviewed, Mineko Iwasaki, "one of Gion's [the geisha section of Kyoto] top geisha in the 1960s and 1970s, opened her Kyoto home to me during May 1992 and corrected my every misconception about the life of a geisha—even though everyone I know who had lived in Kyoto, or who lived there still, told me never to expect such candor."

But I say Mineko Iwasaki would have never let down her face, because she could not possibly let go of her own illusions of her life as a geisha-prostitute. To do that she would have had to realize that she'd been used, completely used, in a patriarchal society. And nothing of that concept comes across in the book. One cannot hold up the illusion that prostitution is in any way romantic.

In the novel he definitely states, from the narrator's point of view, that becoming a geisha in the long run gave Sayuri a better outcome in life than she would have ever had coming from a poor family. How can a woman be a prostitute and feel as if she's in any way in control of her life? The geisha in Golden's book falls in love with a client and in the end marries that client. She goes into a much higher class than the one she was born into, and she lives happily ever after. That's a fairy tale. She marries a father figure, and he saves her from her life. It's great patriarchal bullshit. I mean, maybe becoming a geisha in Japan is one of the few ways—maybe one of the only ways in the old days—that allowed a poor girl to get into a higher class, but even if it was, which I don't doubt, that mere fact makes it patriarchal. The fact that prostitution exists in a society illustrates the force and power of the existence of patriarchy.

To be successful to me means to be happy with what I am doing and to be able to make a reasonable living from what I am doing. To be able to share that kind of life with a partner and to be in a community with like-minded people, where art and beauty are of importance. I think I have some of that now, but I would like to have more time to write.

If you asked me what my fantasy of aging is, I would say, "Wrinkles." No! Just kidding! You know, I know many older and wise people who are not incapacitated in any way whatsoever and are more creative now than they were when they were younger. That's my fantasy of aging: to become wiser and more creative. In our society, we so idolize youth and the young. I think being older is really where it's at. Who wants to be twenty again? The twenties are brutal.

The negative aspects of aging would be something like illness: to get ill or be incapacitated in any way physically or mentally. My analyst is eighty-six years old, and he has a full schedule. He's absolutely incredible. His mind is as sharp as a razor.

I like the vision of the crone. I like the fact that the crone is an old woman who can and does do the unexpected. Some people think this is a negative image, but I think it's a wonderful image. A crone is a woman who's come to complete acceptance of her life, and she has full titleship over her own life. She is not judged. She can say whatever she wants to say, because by that time in life, if she's really lived it and looked at it, whatever she says is worthwhile. To become a crone, you have to have lived a life, and you have to have digested that life. Once you've done that, you have a right to it and a right to talk about it or not talk about it. But you are wise, a wise old woman.

*Pay attention to your feelings. Notice when you don't feel right about a situation; don't write it off. Don't worry about what other people think of you. Don't do things for other people's approval. It's really important not to get caught up in what's trendy, because in the long run it doesn't matter. Figure out what really matters to you. Go for the heart rather than the head. Look at what you're being drawn to do.*

ELISABETH TARG

# Elisabeth Targ

## PROFILE

Elisabeth Targ, a physician, is the program director for the California Medical Center's Breast Cancer Personal Support/Lifestyle Intervention Trial, a group experiment project to determine the effect of alternative healing methods on breast cancer patients. Elisabeth is tall and slender and carries a calmness and quality of presence that befits her years of Tibetan Buddhist meditation. She remembers coming to this project practically kicking and screaming: "This won't work; it's not scientific." Her biggest roadblock to working with such alternative healing methods as yoga, meditation, massage, nutrition, acupuncture, herbs, and dance and art therapies was her skeptical insistence that their efficacy was unproved.

Elisabeth comes from a line of scientists. Her father, Russell, is a physicist and one of the inventors of the laser. He is also legally blind, and perhaps as a result he became fascinated by ESP and psi (parapsychological psychic powers), other means of seeing. With her father as a role model, Elisabeth has been interested in the working of the brain and mind since she was a child and working with him on his scientific experiments at the Stanford Research Institute.

Now as a psychiatrist, she feels the necessity to do research and provide straight answers to patients about all facets of medical care. Eventually circumstances and Elisabeth's curiosity would lead her research into the most difficult and profoundly important area of many people's lives: prayer and spirituality.

In the late 1980s, Elisabeth was working with AIDS patients at UCLA's Neuropsychiatric Institute, involved in a study that showed that group therapy was at least as good as Prozac for treating depression. At about the same time, David Spiegel at Stanford Medical School published his findings that group therapy could dramatically increase life expectancy for women with breast cancer. Elisabeth wondered if the studies proved that providing opportunities for emotional release and social support is what allowed the mind to heal the body, or if there were deeper, unseen connections between people that made the difference.

When her dear friend and godmother, photographer Hella Hammid, was diagnosed with breast cancer, she asked Elisabeth if there was any evidence that spiritual development might help cure her cancer. That was the beginning of a journey that has brought Elisabeth to her current four-year-long project.

At the young age of thirty-eight, Elisabeth has the impressive credentials of being an assistant clinical professor of psychiatry at the University of California, San Francisco, and California Pacific Medical Center. Although she is devoted to her professional work, Elisabeth lives with a man with whom she hopes to have a baby. True to her nature of total engagement and her philosophy of integrating all aspects of her life, she doesn't plan to let go of anything: "I'm convinced that I could take wonderful care of a child and do my work." After reading *The Continuum Concept* by Jean Liedloff, she sees herself taking her baby "absolutely everywhere, to all meetings, on all planes." For this scientist who has embraced a spiritual reality, everything is possible.

# Harmonizing Science and Spirituality

I was very strongly educated in the concept of phenomenology and scientific integrity—that is, that science is an incredible tool for observing the world, and the only way to use it is if you write down exactly what happens and you accept it at face value without necessarily trying to interpret it. Whatever the data showed, they are giving you information. So if you think you really understand something and you do your experiment, and it doesn't happen the way you thought, there's no such thing as "the experiment didn't work." The experiment *always* works. It will always tell you something, and sometimes it tells you you're wrong or this effect isn't as strong as you thought. That's information too.

During medical school, I was very interested in the relationship between mind and body, and I thought that was really simulated by all these other observations. When I started to study psychology and psychopathology in college, I was intrigued with why two different people could be in the same experience and yet come out feeling very differently. I think a kind of pivotal piece of datum that I was given as a college student and really caught my attention was about depression in twin studies that were used to prove that depression is a genetic phenomenon. If you're an identical twin and you suffer from major depression, it's an 85 percent chance that your twin is going to suffer from major depression. I thought, Wow, that means 15 percent of the people don't get depressed even though they have the genetics that should cause them to be depressed; I wonder what's different about them. I wonder if their experience is different or they interpret the experiences differently. Added to that was work by Victor Frankl in a Nazi concentration camp, which saw hundreds of thousands of people go into the concentration camp and come out deeply scarred and traumatized, but a small minority of people didn't. What was different about them? What was different about where they put their attention? Those two realms of thinking were the things that, more than anything else, kind of turned me in a direction that has led to the work that I'm doing now.

I went to medical school because I was interested in mind-body questions, and I felt that if I was going to look at anything in a serious way, I had to understand how the body works. I really had to understand it, not be mystified by it. I got a little bit waylaid because it happened that I really loved working with patients; it was fun for me. For quite some time I thought I would become an internal medicine doctor. I loved staying up late in the hospital, visiting the patients and being involved in their care. I went in assuming I would go into psychiatry, because I really felt there wasn't that much known in psychiatry. To me, that's where all the really interesting questions were that had to do with these early questions that I carried with me: What does it mean to be who we are? Why do some people feel one way and other people feel another way? What does it mean to be connected to people across the globe? It was clear to me that psychiatry had almost nothing to say on any of those subjects. I felt that that was the field in which one would legitimately be asking those questions, so I threw myself into that and into the study of psychiatric phenomenology and treatment.

The work that I'm involved in now is basically saying that maybe optimum health is not represented by what a group of Psych 101 students did on the Minnesota Multiphasic Personality Inventory. Maybe they're actually very constricted and immature. And there's a huge amount of learning that may be possible in terms of the whole continuum of psychospiritual development that might happen afterward. That's really what I'm interested in now. What else is possible? And also how this kind of knowledge of what else might help people who are stuck in fairly well-understood situations like anxieties or depression. About ten years ago, I got involved in something new and controversial, the idea of guided imagery. I started working with women in a locked-in patient psychiatric unit, where most of them were, I believe, incorrectly labeled as psychotic or schizophrenic. I became interested in their stories and found that actually spending time with these people would show that many of them had been through extraordinary experiences, most of which would terrify any of the psychiatrists or the psychiatric residents who were working with them. If anybody would actually pay attention to what some of these women had been through on the streets of San Francisco in terms of hiding in the garbage can watching their friend

being raped, watching somebody getting killed, getting shot at themselves—
*every day*—they might have a different perspective on the patient's behavior.
I spent a lot of time talking to the residents about it. For example, I'd say,
"You think there's something wrong with this woman because she's screaming in the halls, but it may be just what she needs to be doing. Screaming in
the halls may be the best that she can be doing with her experience. You
need to consider what you would be doing if that had happened to you even
once, let alone every day for the past two years." We developed a whole unit
culture on this idea of talking to people and hearing the stories. We spent a
lot of time with the stories—a lot of time in our own imagination with
what it would really be like to be in these situations. That sounds very ordinary, but I'm sorry to say that it's a pretty novel approach in psychiatry.

The other thing that we started doing was working with guided imagery tapes. That was so out-of-bounds in the psychiatric department that
I actually had to write a formal doctor's order for any of the nurses to be
comfortable with one of the patients having imagery or meditation tapes. I
was struck by the richness of the inner environment that these tapes opened
up for some of our patients—the power of that inner validation of her perhaps spiritual, perhaps archetypal, perhaps deeply wise or intuitive inner self
and that there were tremendous resources in each one of these women.
When somebody acknowledged this inner strength or somebody helped
her know about it (because she did not always know it), there was a tremendous relaxation and a recommitment to her own healing in a way that
she could then start to engage much more with what we were trying to
offer in our standard psychiatric way. Things became much less scary. But it
really required *our* going into *their* world as they went into their world and
their being acknowledged as people. The trickier question is, What is spirituality? For whatever reason, I was intrigued. I saw how people within the
spiritual community and spiritual traditions were working with the very
same things that I had been observing in what to my mind was straight science or straight psychiatry. Spirituality seemed to be something about inner
resources and something about connection. So I decided I would investi-
gate it. I think that was my scientific training that prompted me: don't write
something off because you don't understand it; go and observe it at least

once. So I did. I spent four months visiting spiritual communities, reading spiritual literature, trying out different practices, trying out different meditations and imageries and prayers, and listening to teachers. I was definitely impressed that there is a describable experience and describable set of values and cosmology that people in many different traditions are exploring and participating in.

That was as far as I went with this. In all these different traditions, people are saying the same thing: that they feel connected, that when they really enter into this connection, it is a profoundly peaceful and blissful experience that has something to do with letting go of their particular investment in the story of who they are. When they are invested in that, whether it's a good story or a bad story, they tend to feel worse than when they go into this kind of relaxation. There's tremendous joy and there's tremendous suffering in this path. Furthermore, it seems to be clear that for people in different traditions, these experiences were more available when they were quiet, when they stopped their thinking. It was also clear that there was a kind of cosmology, a kind of explanation, that teachers were offering to people that was helpful to them—that when they were quiet by themselves, their experience could also be confusing and not necessarily beneficial. These were just observations. It's almost as if I was the science nerd in Spiritland. At the same time, when I was taught to have some of these experiences too, I was intrigued. As I spent more time with these traditions, I also felt that I could be more present for the next step of what they were talking about. So there were things I would hear that maybe ten years before I would have just written off and might have been anxiety provoking or irritating to me. Instead, after I had spent time with these communities, it was meaningful and intriguing.

It had a really profound effect on me. Tibetan practice was more accessible to me than others, like Zen practice or other religious practice or just plain mindfulness. That's because Tibetan practice is so unbelievable and strange that there's no way to wrap your mind around it. Some people call it the Roman Catholicism of Buddhism—full of colors and deities and strange things. At a certain point you just have to give up: either you're going to do it, or you're not going to do it. I decided to do it. It really gave me an experience, which I don't completely understand, of opening up. I think it creates a relaxation and an increased awareness and availability to something more about empathy and connection. It was through that practice that I acquired the tools to develop a program of spiritual exploration for women with breast cancer.

It gave me a spiritual practice that I've continued, and I've moved in other directions as well. But it also helped show me what it would mean and how to understand those practices from the inside, having actually practiced them, and then seeing how extremely similar they are to Christian healing practices and Jewish healing practices and nondenominational healing practices and new age imagery healing practices, and how very, very much related they are. But it was important to have developed a practice to do it, because there are huge pitfalls, which I see also. I think that the new age spirituality that's available is really helpful for about 20 percent of the people who find it. A huge number of people just write it off; they don't like it, it's nonsense. People come to it for different reasons. Some people come to it, and it becomes a path of real exploration and opening for them. I see a lot of other people coming to it as candy and a way of dissociating themselves from pain and basically arresting their growth. I'm concerned about that diversion. Lots of sweetness and light and a pink cocoon wrapped around their shoulders block them out from growth that they really need to do. Other people it just irritates. It was helpful for me to work within a more developed tradition with a teacher who could really talk to me and say, "You're miserable? Good, that's how you're supposed to be right now. Keep going." That was the launching place for me to move into all other kinds of work since then. I was interested in the question of new age guilt—basically all of these teachings that are available now to women with breast cancer: "You should pray, you should meditate, and you should visualize." And there are so many books out that say, "You got your breast cancer because it's a women's issue, and you were too giving," or "You weren't giving enough," or "You had mother issues." I'm really worried about this; I've seen it be very detrimental to people. Yet at the same time, almost every spiritual tradition offers a perspective that says mishaps, even difficulties, may offer teaching in one way or another. So we ask women if "you believe your illness is meant to teach you something." We had the hypothesis that that actually would be associated with a worse outcome—that they would be feeling guilty or punished. Actually it had almost the opposite effect. Women who felt that their illness was meant to teach them something were actually doing better psychologically than women who didn't. At the same time, a small subset of women who felt that their illness was a punishment were doing worse. That information we have so far.

In one project I met a researcher from the Institute of Noetic Sciences who was interested in the concept of psychic healing and prayer. He said, "Somebody really ought to do a formal study on that." I said, "I don't think that'll work because the mind-body connection is so powerful and the hope and expectation factor is so important. That's what we're cultivating in spirituality, isn't it?" This idea of really using kind of a magic, a nonlocal effect over distance, I thought, was basically out of bounds. But I said, "I think we could study it and put this thing to rest."

He and I set out to do a formal study of the effects of prayer on people with AIDS. We did a successful pilot study. It was amazing to everybody. The largeness of effect in a very small sample was amazing. We saw 40 percent of the patients who didn't get the healing die, and nobody in the treatment group died. It really caught everybody's attention. As we reviewed the data, we started to think about other explanations. We needed to plug all these holes with possible other explanations and do it again. So we did it again. At this point, we haven't found any holes to plug. We did it again, this time with forty patients. We involved healers from every spiritual tradition: Christians, Jews, Buddhist healers, Native American shamanic healers, energy healers, secular healers, contemplative healers, evangelical healers with a fourth-grade education—everybody. We found even stronger results and published them in the *Western Journal of Medicine.* For me, that was kind of the last straw. I'm going to have to accept these data, and I'm going to accept the 150 other studies done by other people that found similar results to these.

At the California Pacific Medical Center Health and Healing Clinic, where we do most of our research studies, in addition to mainstream medicine, we also have herbal medicine, acupuncture, and homeopathy and hands-on healing and spiritual direction. I work in the clinic two days a week as a psychiatrist. While I continue to work with medications and I do hand out my share of Prozac and other things, I tend to be much more likely to hold visions of patients for themselves and with themselves as basically intrinsically perfect just the way they are. Whatever is happening for them is an important and necessary part of their evolution. They are not damaged. They are not pathological. They are who they need to be, and everybody is different. We can work together if they have other ways of being and other things that they want for themselves in their lives; we can work together to help them achieve more flexibility in life, but not to say that they are sick or that they are wrong. I think more than anything else, that is the change that has occurred in my practice of psychiatry as a result of the exposure to all the spiritual work.

The other thing I do now is adapt many of the tools from spiritual practice, which are various trainings in awareness, concentration, and heart-opening practices—especially of basic meditation, feeling awareness practices, loving kindness meditation. These include holding a certain optimism in terms of forgiveness and considerations of the nature of mortality. All of those things I brought into my medical practice as a result of the observations within our research. So I do that two days a week. The rest of the time I run this program and direct that institute, where we are now doing studies of the outcomes in that clinic to see how people do there. Some of the really basic questions people were asking at the hospital (where we are studying the use of massage therapy) are: "Well, do they like it? Are people going to be offended by massage? Are they going to be freaked out by it?" So we did really basic studies to find out—well, actually, they love it. Eighty percent of the people in the hospital have never had massage before, which is amazing to me.

In the more personal realm, I have a boyfriend; we've lived together for four years. We met in a meditation group. We sat together in silence for a full year before we ever went out on our first date, so we got to know each other very well. He's a physicist doing research in consciousness. We really want to have children, and I'm kind of worried about it, being thirty-eight. It hasn't happened yet, although we just started to try in the last six months. I'm convinced that I could take wonderful care of a child and do my work. My plan would be to keep my child with me all the time as much as I could. I feel that a lot of my work is really flexible. In this environment, it would be really easy to have a little baby here. A good friend of mine at the Institute of Noetic Sciences just had a baby; she's the research director there. She takes that baby with her absolutely everywhere—to all meetings, on all planes—so I see it can be done. That would be my plan.

The other thing is I'm really trying to keep a balance in our lives. About two and a half or three years ago, Mark and I joined up with a group of people in Sonoma, before anybody started worrying about Y2K, for a land-based community up there where we have forty acres and people have built little dwellings. We found it because we went up there just knowing that we wanted to find a place up in Sonoma, put up a little yurt for retreat, and then by a series of connect coincidences, we found this group of people. We have our little sixty-foot yurt in the woods in Forestville. We try and go there as often as possible, which is usually two weekends a month, to have a sort of other little life there. No plumbing. Only a little wood stove to heat it. Big organic gardens there. An opportunity to be in a really different relation to earth and other people. A lot of what I do here in this program is actually really based on things I learned about living in community there. We have community meetings in the old consciousness-raising style of the sixties and seventies. That is how that group of ten people functions, who have to live together, and it's a group of people very drawn to earth spirituality in a way that's not a specific spiritual practice community. Our community up there makes decisions by holding hands in a circle and everybody speaking from their heart, using the council practice and all of that. A lot of what I've learned there intermixes to be part of the programs here.

I grew up always wanting to have a land-based, intentional community outside the city. Ever since I was about seven or eight years old, every single weekend my parents and I would go with a group of eight or nine people from different families, looking for land, usually in the Santa Cruz Mountains. It took them fifteen years to find a place and by then I was already in college. My college admission essay to Stanford was about land-based community, including organic gardening and how to make decisions in community. That eventually happened, but in a really difficult way. Little by little, a lot of the families fell away, and it became my parents and one other couple buying this big piece of land, and they ended up selling lots on it to other people to try to make a community. But by that time, the land had appreciated so much that the people who could afford to buy into it were people who had a much more corporate mentality, and it evolved into a nightmare. Basically what happened is our new "neighbors" decided they didn't want to let us have organic gardens on the land.

Eventually the question of the garden ended up in court, and after five years in court, my mother finally won. Then she died. She died of a stroke six weeks after she won the right to her garden. I'm completely convinced it was because of that; she was only sixty years old and in perfect health. She was a farmer, in the Women's Health Initiative, ate a no-fat diet, walked her land every day, pushed a plow. I remember saying to her in the midst of this court battle, when she was under so much stress, "Mom, I can't tell you how grateful I am to you for doing this—what you've created for us and for our family forever after. But I want you to know that I'm not sure it's worth it. This is too much stress; people get strokes from things like this." And she did, a year ago. It's been an incredible tragedy for our whole family and for me in particular as her daughter. I felt there were a lot of unfinished things between us. It's been really hard.

From this experience, I learned about the importance of communication, but it was really about the people. The people on my mother's land made their living doing corporate takeovers and suing people, as we later found out. That was actually their profession—corporate takeovers and suits. Many of the people there had made their whole livelihood this way, and some of them were millionaires. The people I live with up north are hippies; they don't have any money at all. That's perfect. Everybody gets along just fine. Everybody is willing to take their life savings, whatever it is, and put it into the land. We talk about everything we want to do, but there's a joint ethic. Yes, organic gardening is really useful.

There was always a project in our home. My father was doing the remote viewing. I worked with him from the time I was in high school; before that, I was involved in his experiments: as his research assistant and later as his coexperimenter. We published papers together. My experience in Palo Alto in the sixties and seventies when I was growing up was full of exciting opportunity and ideas.

Everybody I knew had a start-up company in their living room or a research institute of some sort in their kitchen. There were projects going on constantly. Our home address had our house and Interactive Sciences Inc., it was also Bay Research Laboratories, it was ESP Laboratories. Even though my father was working at Scientific Research Institute and my mother was working in the school district, still there were all these other little things happening. It was very lively and very intellectually—but not spiritually—oriented. It was all toward figuring things out and making things better, but always with a very humanistic intent. My parents were interested in humanism, interested in human potential, growth, educating children. My mother had *amazing* projects going even before the garden stuff.

What are preventive measures for breast cancer? I don't have an answer that is based in my scientific research. The closest thing I could say out of my own research is to maintain really good awareness of your body and to learn to manage stress as much as possible, because we know it does affect the immune system. But I am cautious about saying that, because I don't want people to think I'm saying that because you are stressed out, it caused your breast cancer, which really isn't the case. But I think you can basically hedge your bets if you can decrease stress.

The other thing is to eat organic. I'm sorry to say we have so little information in general. At this point there's so much evidence about the various toxins in our environment; you have to drink organic milk if you're going to drink milk, and you should eat a low-fat diet. That's the best information out there. If there's one thing it's to spend the extra money at the grocery store and eat organic.

Our garden up in Forestville has plenty of vegetables, and so does my mom's garden, because we've kept that going. It's being farmed incredibly by a woman who was the bailiff in the trial, who was so impressed with my mom that she got special permission from the court to work on the farm, even though you're not supposed to fraternize with the litigants. She's been working on it for a whole year. I get really beautiful vegetables from there. My mom's favorite flower was sunflower, and we planted about a thousand of them and take them to market.


Advice to other women in their thirties? Don't eat hamburgers. Ha! Gosh, a lot of things. I don't know quite how to package it. Really pay attention to your feelings. It's almost like the data thing again: notice when you don't feel right about a situation. Don't write that off. Pay attention to it, and really explore who you are. Don't worry about what other people think about you. Don't do things for other people's approval. Don't assume that the world now is your reward in any way. Figure out who you are personally. Something I've been doing ever since I was a kid, and I don't know why, is to ask, "What if I was born two hundred years ago? Then what?" It's really important not to get caught up in the environment of what's trendy and what's being offered to you right now, because in the long run it doesn't matter. Figure out what really matters to you. Go for the heart rather than the head. Look what you're being drawn to do. Don't be so critical of yourself. That's a really big one: don't be so critical of yourself. It's not worth it. And you're really fine. There's a reason that things are happening the way they are.

I think we're all part of something, and I think each one of us is growing. We grow slowly. That's another thing—not pushing it, not being hard on oneself. I regret so many things every day. It's been so helpful for me to say, "I guess I couldn't do it right this time," and then I take it a little further and say, "Why not? What was going on? I guess I had to do that one more time, and let's see what happens next time." It's a healthful thing. What are all the things I can understand about why I did it that way instead of the way that I now think would have been so much better? I'll check into that."

I know my own schedule may sound pretty stressful, but I work only four days a week. I take Fridays off, which helps me catch up. All the things I'm doing are things I want to be doing anyway, so it's not as if I have to go do my real life somewhere else. All day long, I get to talk about everything I want to talk about. That's probably the biggest saving grace. I do get stressed out. I have to make careful choices and turn down a lot of things that are offered and try to pay attention to what is the full value in what I'm doing now. My boyfriend went to this amazing conference in Costa Rica last month, and I could have gone for free and it would have been really great. But that was just going to take me away from what I'm doing here. If there is going to be any real depth and kind of relaxation into my work here at the Breast Cancer Program, I need to stay here. I'll be happier here than I would be if I were running around Costa Rica, even though it would be great to go. When I do make it up to our Forestville land, I try to really let myself be there.

When I got to my thirties, there was a switch. That was the end of following the path of my education and doing the work that both my mother and my father had been doing. It was the time when I came to find out something about my own self. I incorporated my own self into the work and the training and the kind of life I'd had before. In a lot of ways, that's when, if my life was a song, my thirties is when the variation on a theme began. Through my teens and twenties, I was really very much still working within my family, living within my family values and considerations and perspectives. Then when I got into my thirties, I started to add something, contribute much more of my own, find out something more about who I was and to put that into the mix. There was a change—maybe more than for other people because I was in school for so long and was in an environment while I was growing up that was so enriching.

There are two sides to that. The good news is that it's extremely enriching and exciting. The bad news is that you can kind of get lost in it and not know who *you* are. There was a risk for me of not finding out who I was as an individual. After I went away, ended my residency, there started to be more moments when I would get angry at medicine and not like it and to disagree with it. Research and medicine were all things that I had really been taught that I was going to enjoy and that I was going to respect. When

I found that I didn't, I sort of had my own little private mini-fit by refusing to go off to the National Institutes of Health and do a fellowship. I finished my residency and instead came up to San Francisco and started working in the psychiatric emergency room. I just wanted to have a life. I was working only two days a week, and that was when I had enough space in my life to try to figure out what actually was meaningful to me. I started doing things not because I was supposed to. I had completed everything I was supposed to do. I had completed getting a few papers published, I had completed my medical school and my residency, so in a sense, now the rest of it's for me. It wasn't that I went off on a search. It was that I was done; I wasn't fulfilling anybody's expectations anymore.

I wanted to see what would happen. I started following my own path, which, as it turned out, was always leading me naturally back into communication with people and wanting to be more involved in various kinds of study groups and exploratory groups. But now it was because I wanted to, not because it was expected of me or because it was a particular railroad track that I'd been put on. That switch was important for the thirties.

I was recently at a baby shower for a baby whom my mother had really prayed for to be born from a woman who was forty, a woman she'd been close to and encouraged. She was a woman who had been through all sorts of in vitro fertilization and everything. The baby was born after my mother died, and as part of the baby shower, all of the women were asked to offer a blessing for the baby—a gift that their mother had given them that they could give to the baby. The one from my mom was manifesting vision. You can really make your big dreams come true, and you don't have to be put down; you don't have to believe it when people tell you, "That's not possible." She had always done it; she modeled that. The other thing she always reminded me: Even if you're doing things that seem unusual or extraordinary and sometimes people might be very impressed, there is really nothing for them to be impressed about. When you're doing it, all you do is just put one foot in front of the other. When you're in it, it's really just ordinary, but it's just a matter of doing what you're going to do and not worrying about it too much—not worrying if it sounds as if it's really hard or out of reach. You just do it.

That's always been my experience, so I ended up in some fields that people think are unusual or wonder how it can happen. My sense is that it was a matter of just doing it—not living by other people's image of what's supposed to happen.

*In my thirties I've come to master self-image as a feeling state.
For example, beauty is a feeling of well-being; therefore, it's not
necessarily how I look to others, which was important in my twenties, but how my body feels. If I feel beautiful, I am. This perspective is much different from measuring up to an ideal or image state,
which is an abstraction and has nothing to do with who I am or
the reality of my life.*

CHARLENE WOLF

# Charlene Wolf

## PROFILE

Some women are natural-born mothers and Charlene Wolf is one of them. Her loveliness is part of, but not limited to, the fact of her motherhood. Char, or Mama Char, as I call her, has three children and just turned thirty-seven. I have known her for only two years, but I have greatly benefited from her calm, nurturing presence. She became pregnant shortly after we met, and I had the privilege of watching her body and moods change during those nine months.

Char, like many other women in their thirties, wants it all—marriage, children, career—and she is at least two-thirds there. Being married to a successful doctor who practices in the area of weight loss and antiaging in Orange County, California, allows her the benefit of financial security and to spend time with her children rather than having to work to support them. That's why it is even more admirable that Char also pursues a rich academic life in psychology and mythological studies and plans to establish her own career after her children reach school age.

In our interview Char discusses the miracle of motherhood and how she happily juggles all her interests.

**125**

## Living a Full Life

I grew up in a quiet California suburban neighborhood. As soon as I reached eighteen, I left the concrete and planned communities of inland Orange County and moved closer to the ocean; I wanted to be part of the carousing beach life. I spent my twenties sailing and working for a charter boat club, which was extremely physical and delightful. I inherited my father's mechanical ability and love of machines, and this proved to be useful in my passion for boats. Working outside and sailing for so many years, I gained a deep respect for nature and an understanding of the consistency of change. I found this life intellectually stimulating as well; sailors, besides loving the pleasures of wind and wine, are well-read freethinkers.

I married quite young, at twenty. Five years later I gave birth to my first child, Max. Just after his first birthday, I went through an internal upheaval. The calm and happy life I held dear was replaced by a wanderlust for expanded experience and possibility. My marriage ended, and even though we agreed to dual custody of our son, my ex-husband took over a larger portion of Max's care. The separation from my son was agonizing, yet at the time, it seemed a more stable arrangement for Max. The pain and difficulty my son has experienced in living in two households is one of the reasons I've made parenting a priority and spiritual discipline in my thirties.

Two years after my divorce, I remarried, ended my boating career and began a new life, which included returning to school to complete my undergraduate degree in anthropology at the University of California at Irvine. My daughter, Erika, was born toward the end of my studies. She was just learning to walk at my graduation. After a four-year break. I went on to pursue a master's in mythological studies. In my second year of graduate work, I gave birth to my third child, Dylan Rumi, who is now one year old. All three of my children were planned, as were my degrees.

I view the work of my thirties to be about balancing my commitments to loving and raising my children in full partnership with my husband, Gregory, and exercising my intellect in my studies. Both endeavors bring to me a full life.

My interest in myth goes back to a high school English class. The teacher presented myth in such a passionate and embodied way that the class became one of the strongest memories from my teen years. Anthropology has a subfield in folklore, yet it wasn't until I found a graduate program that focused on world myths—their interpretations and what they have to say about the human condition—that I felt at home. The visionaries who led me deeper into this field of study after my initial opening were the mythologist Joseph Campbell and the archetypal psychologist James Hillman.

During my graduate studies, Ginnete Paris, a professor, made a definite impact on deepening my understanding of ancient Greek mythology and the profound understanding its religion had on developing and understanding human psychology and current popular culture. The focus area of my studies concentrated on the universal and archetypal nature of love, sex, and the dynamic tension between female and male. This research gave me an expanded understanding and deeper appreciation of my own erotic nature and the tremendous power inherent in the union between the sexes.

Deepening the quality of my commitment to being a parent is another kind of work. My husband and I have discovered a way of parenting that is generative as opposed to exhaustive. In all powerful and valuable work, one has mentors. Ba and Josette Luvmour, the founders of Natural Learning Rhythms, have developed a way to work with parents, children, and families that views the world from a child's developmental abilities, strengths, and perspective. When one relates to a child as having inherent wisdom, one is aligned with a child's deepest needs. I believe that if we as a culture are to begin raising our children in a healthy way, we need to understand a child's world and way of thinking rather than impose ours on theirs. In this way, we also will be transformed, and in the end, given the condition the world and our children are in, a cultural transformation must happen.

The Luvmours have a holistic learning center, Encompass, outside Sacramento, California. Initially I was attracted to their work in order to understand my eldest son's conflicts. Since he was so young during the divorce, the trauma did not surface until he was nine. My daughter was also in need of firmer boundaries, which my husband and I were struggling to create and maintain. We were pretty much a mess when we arrived at their family camp. Three years later, I am now proud to say that many acknowledge my mothering skills. I'm proud of my hard-earned new abilities, yet a supportive husband and friends make or break a great mother. In addition, our families of origin are loving and supportive. The difference between my experience as a mother now and when I was twenty-five is that I feel less alone now. Motherhood has an element of leisure to it when you allow yourself to meander with your children in play. I have a large, satisfying group of mature women who share the same experiences and responsibilities inherent in motherhood as well as the leisure time.

As a mother you don't have a boss who oversees your performance. It is important to surround yourself with people who can openly express concerns, fears, and victories. With my best friend, Hanna, we build on our strengths and work out areas in need of improvement as mothers. I have learned to carry enough humility and self-confidence to admit weaknesses and alter damaging behavior that nurtures neither myself or my children.


My ability to move through fear of change and transform is an earned asset, nurtured first in sailing and then during my three labors. The first time I sailed to Catalina Island, about a twenty-six-mile sail from the mainland, I could not see the land or the island, and I began to question my knowledge of navigation. Instead of bringing my terror to the forefront, I moved my fear aside. I looked at the faces of my friends, who trusted me. I knew that if I showed any terror, I'd have another issue to deal with; for their emotional well-being and the greater good of the journey, courage was demanded. I was nineteen at the time and have carried this initiation since. In a culture where initiations are not instituted, I believe we create our own and wear them like a badge, which can be called up as a resource. This resource of moving my fear aside was invaluable during the births of my three children. I experienced all three labors without medication. I read in my anthropology literature about a group of women from Central America who gave birth in the United States and were appalled at the thought of anesthetizing the pain of labor. For them it was an honor, a badge of courage, a memory to be used as a future resource. That struck a cord with me. I would say that anytime I get into a situation that requires moving fear or pain aside, I draw on these experiences.

At least once a year or sometimes more, I take a weekend by myself away from the responsibilities of my family and other projects. I feel most alive when I am well rested. I laugh more easily, and creative ideas flow. I love to receive massage, rolfing, acupuncture—anything involving the body. I am a very kinesthetic lover.

In my thirties I've come to master self-image as a feeling state. For me, beauty is no longer about how I look to others, which was important in my twenties, as much as it is a feeling of well-being. How does my body feel? How do I feel? If I feel beautiful, I am. If I'm tired, run down, in need of exercise, or have overindulged, this lack of balance shows. This perspective is much different from measuring up to an ideal or image, which is an abstraction and has nothing to do with who I am or the reality of my life. I believe that to heal women's self-image issues, we need to deconstruct the inherent cultural meanings individually and redefine self-image with new myths or personal values.

On my thirtieth birthday I hired a Russian band that played American rock songs like "La Bamba" on traditional folk instruments. It was quite a large and Dionysian celebration. For my most recent birthday, my husband and I spent an evening in an expensive suite in Los Angeles. We had wine and shopped and then spent the rest of the afternoon in bed. We ate great meals and had great sex and rediscovered ourselves as a couple distinct from our role as parents. In this way, we replenish our relationship, which can be so easily neglected in the overwhelming day-to day-life of raising a family.

My marriage is a religious stew. I come from Catholicism and my husband from Judaism. Max is being raised Catholic, and we had a bris for Dylan. Because of the mixed marriage, we have sought other nonspecific forms of spiritual expression. I have an image of my husband and me living out our elderly years on Maui as an old, eccentric, and in-love couple eating mangoes, tofu, and flax seed.

Perhaps the most important lesson I've learned in my life is to be loyal and loving to others and surround myself with loyal and loving people. In this way, most of life's challenges turn into blessings. My advice to other women who have visions or passions and want to pursue them is: Know your passion, make a plan, and stick to it like a bulldog. Let the process of its actualization become your life.

I desire to nurture my children with the same tenacity. My eldest son is creatively gifted. I took him to Paris when he was ten. Just the two of us. We walked all over the city and explored the Louvre and EuroDisney. It was an incredible bonding time for us.

I look forward to watching my daughter grow into a woman. She wants to be a singer, and I plan to start her with a vocal coach this year. Recently I was listening to a radio station playing music from the seventies and eighties, and I realized how silenced and unrepresented the female voice was in music when I was young. Now most stations play an even mix of male and female vocalists. The expansion of female vocalists, I believe, is a microcosm of the overall experience women have in the latter part of this century. My daughter, who identifies with female vocalists, is also under the care of a female physician and a female dentist. She has no awareness of what the women's movement did for her. What was once considered leaps are now an everyday occurrence in her world. This is a remarkable gift.

The thirties for me are about laying the foundation for the coming decades. My twenties were about sailing and parties and play. My thirties are about healing my ability as a mother, taking seriously the raising of my children, and pursuing my passion for myth. My forties will be about cohesion—the melding of my studies, experiences as a mother, maturity, and life experiences and the power inherent, which will turn these seemingly disparate parts into a whole and contributing force.

We have to work hard to understand ourselves, so a lot of it
is about doing the work. Doing the work. You can bitch and
moan about your life, and that's OK if you're doing the work.
If you're not doing the work, then it's difficult to get to a place
where you're accepting, because there's always doubt, there's always
wonder, and there's always fear.

TERRY SCHNEIDER

# Terry Schneider

## PROFILE

As they say in ultrarunning, you run the first fifty miles of a hundred-mile race with your legs and the second with your heart. And Terry Schneider, a World-Class Ironman Triathlete, is all heart. I was fortunate to meet Terry, who also excels as a personal coach, when I was thinking about doing a women's triathlon myself. It was thanks to her inspiration and "tough love" during my four-month period of training with her that I fulfilled my dream.

Terry raced on a world-class level for ten years as a professional tri-athlete. Among her notable performances are three top-five finishes in the Hawaii Ironman Triathlon World Championships. She has been a top contender in all twenty-two Ironmans and four Ironman World Series she has completed. As a member of the world-famous team SCAR, Terry has competed internationally in a dozen adventure races, including four Eco-Challenges, the ESPN X-Games, and the Mild Seven Outdoor Quest. Along with her twenty years of experience in triathlon, running, weight training, aerobic instruction, nutrition counseling, and motivational

speaking, Terry, a certified fitness specialist and a myofascial release therapist, has a B.S. in exercise physiology and is completing an M.A. in sports
psychology.

Terry considers herself a "perpetual glass-is-half-full person." She says
that even hours after her ordeal in a Western States 100 race, she can see
the wonders in the race: "Running through wilderness areas in the Sierras
at eight thousand feet with views of the valleys and lakes below is an un-
paralleled experience. How lucky I am to be able to take this on. How
fortunate that I can toe the line at one of the toughest one-day races in
the world and soak up the wonders of the task and the course. This is a
brutal and stunningly beautiful course, which makes it all the more intriguing in my book."

Terry seems to come from the premise that human beings are really
good people. And what we need to do is learn how to let that shine: "We
all have it in us. I coach that way. Everyone's an athlete, and all I need to
do is facilitate that aspect of them to come out and shine. We have it in us
already. We're all beautiful people and we're all physically wonderful, and
it's just about letting those things shine and come out—and accept the
good things and not be so hard on ourselves all the time."

## Tough Love

Western States was the name of the race that I did last year, the
prestigious one hundred miler—probably the most well-known
one hundred miler in the world. It starts in Squaw Valley. I had
a problem at mile 62; I pulled my quad muscle. I had to walk the last 38
miles and I finished the race, in about twenty-nine and a half hours. I don't
know if it was ironic, but in a sense as an athlete, I've come full circle, and as
a woman in a lot of ways. You get a little bit older, you gain perspective,
you're in relationships, you learn from those as a woman. From the athlete

perspective, it's the same thing: you learn from mistakes you made and the successes you've had—things like that.

Most of the ultraruns are trail running. They have some road races, but the more popular ones are off-road, on trails, so not only are you doing the distance, you're doing incredibly difficult terrain—really tough. In Western States, we do something like twenty-two thousand feet of climbing during the whole course and about the same amount of descending. Pretty amazing, but the course is just gorgeous. We leave Squaw Valley, go up to Immigrant Pass, then basically traverse along a ridge line for a really long time, and then start to drop down. The race finishes in Auburn. Really, really pretty; very tough race.

If you look at the race from an outsider's perspective, you could say, "Terry, you got an injury; that really sucks." But it was an interesting personal experience for me to go through that and to finish with an injury. I saw different sides of myself that I'd never seen before. My drive to finish was beyond anything that was conscious. I was so driven—sort of possessed—to finish this race, even though I was literally dragging one leg behind, hobbling along, and I finished the race. It was fascinating for me to be in that process. I almost felt as if I didn't have control over it, and I was just kind of driving myself forward. I learned a lot from it; it was a really rewarding experience for me.

Where does that drive come from? This is the million-dollar question. If you were to ask my mother, she would say I was born that way. When I was younger, I never considered myself hugely talented, the natural athlete. I do have a lot of natural talent—more so than many other folks—but I've always considered myself a hard worker. I'm very motivated and go at work hard. Those are my attributes. And I'm also tough mentally. That's another thing I have going for me. So I always thought anyone could do what I do and be successful like I am, but after coaching a lot of people and seeing adults from all levels of their life and in different stages, I realize that's not really true. I have some special thing inside that allows me to be focused and organized and totally driven to reach goals that I set for myself. Everything else in my life will be put aside in order for me to accomplish that. Not very many people have that. I've coached a lot of athletes, and I very rarely see that kind of drive.

I've always been that way—since I was a kid. It's partly the competitive thing, but I think it goes beyond that. Most athletes say they want to win and be competitive, but it's more about a feel for the activity that keeps them going—that they really enjoy the sport and they enjoy the flow of being in the moment and all that that entails. That's what drives me. I enjoy the activity, but I learn a lot about myself by doing races.

I'm a very social, outgoing person, and I consider myself extroverted, but as I get older, that becomes less so. The more intense things that I do in my life beyond mainstream—and especially as a woman—the more I become isolated, because a lot of people don't really understand what I do and they can't relate to it. So I become selective about who I choose to have in my life and be close to and hang out with. So it's kinda tough, especially as a woman. Most of my life, a career besides my sporting career has gone by the wayside a little bit more than I'd like it to. Now I'm making a shift. My racing is becoming more personal. I'm still competitive when I do events, but it's not so much about winning as it is just about experiencing things. I'm starting to focus more on career. I feel that I haven't hit my potential or gotten even close to it in reference to career. I'm exploring sports psychology, and I'm not sure exactly what I want to do with that. But it's something I'm exploring and have a lot of thoughts and ideas about and will formulate it as I go down the road. I have a lot of ideas; it's just a matter of figuring out how to execute them.

That's exciting and scary at the same time because there's a part of me that goes, *I'm thirty-seven years old, and I've been doing sports all my life, and I've gotten a lot out of it, and I wouldn't change anything. But now I'm here, and I realize you can't do everything all at once, and therefore my career from a nonathletic perspective has hurt a little bit. I have to learn to accept that that's the way it is.* When you're an athlete, you focus and dedicate your life to that. There isn't time to do everything.

The thing I don't give myself credit for is that I have to remember that the career I'm moving into is related to the sport that I've done. All my experience is allowing me to have the reputation, to have the business that I have now.

I feel comfortable with what I've done in my life. I could say that if I died tomorrow, I would feel I've had a really full, complete life. I definitely don't want to die tomorrow, but I can say that. I'm one of those people who goes for the gusto; I really put myself out there. If I want to do something, I think, *What do I need to attain that goal?* It's never been, *Maybe I shouldn't do that because I'm a woman* or *I'm afraid to do that.* I have fears, but I learn what I need to do to overcome the fear and to be able to move forward.

What I see in folks I coach is fear, and often that's about the element of the unknown. What I try and do is—let's say they're afraid of swimming in the ocean. What we need to do is find a safe way for them to try to make that happen. When I started doing adventure racing, I had this terrifying fear of mountaineering—the rappelling and ascending things that we do. I'm not afraid of heights. What I realized was that I didn't understand the equipment enough to trust that it was going to keep me safe. The first race I did, we had a limited amount of time for me to learn the skills and then go execute the race. I'm out there in the race thinking, *How do I know this thing is gonna hold onto the rope for me?* I didn't feel comfortable that I had the skills to do it properly, that I wasn't going to hurt myself. I can now assess a situation where, *OK, we're doing a rappel off this cliff; I can look at the anchor of the rope and go, "Is that safe?"* If it is, then I know it's OK: I know how to rappel, the anchor is safe; therefore all I need to do is execute this. There is still the fear of walking off the edge of a cliff. Who wouldn't have it? Rock climbers say it's healthy to have that kind of fear to keep you alert. I've seen people—and I've done it myself—just spin out of control with fear. You have to look at your options. You have fear; therefore, you need to look at what is it specifically that makes you afraid and how you can learn about it.

Swimming in the ocean, some people are afraid of the fact that they can't see the bottom. So maybe they need to learn about what's on the bottom, what kind of wildlife are out here, and what kinds of things could potentially happen, and get a better understanding. We're always going to have that; as human beings, we often will go to that negative place. You'll be out there swimming, and all of a sudden you'll start thinking about sharks, and you can't get that thought out of your head. So then what you have to do is figure out a way to reframe. That's what they call it in sports psychology. Change your thought process, and make it into something different.

I'm thinking of focusing some research in my studies on fear and women in particular. There's a whole history behind why women are afraid of things.

It's interesting to me. You could almost say that we're taught to be afraid. As a woman, it's an admirable trait to have fear. I don't know if that's the way you would define it, but there's a lot behind that: safety issues—just going out and being safe in public. We should be fearful of that rather than say we should be cautious; maybe we take it a step further, and it becomes a fearful thing. But we're supposed to be the weaker sex, the victim, so in a sense we've been programmed to show fear. We take that into our lives. I see strong, intelligent women who want to change that. They have that in them, but they aren't quite sure how to change it because it's almost this thing they've kind of dragged along with them all these years. What I've noticed is that if women can take on challenges in *safe* ways (that's important), then they will learn to have confidence and to do things that they feel competent in that will carry through to their whole life.

I've never been afraid for some reason, and I've always gone after things I wanted, and therefore I have this megaquantity of confidence to draw from. It's not an ego thing; it's just factual. I've had a lot of successes, and I've had a lot of failures that I've learned from, so therefore I have confidence in the fact that I've been able to acknowledge defeat and learn from those defeats, and overcome them, and then move forward. I think that's where confidence comes from. Women need to take things on that help them to learn confidence, and then the fears will start to dissipate and they'll be able to move that into other aspects of their life.

We compare ourselves to others. I try to get people to move away from that because I don't really believe that to work to your potential as an athlete is about comparing yourself to others, because all we have is what we have. It's like you have your body; that's all you have, so there's no point in comparing yourself to others. But what about looking at what *you* can do for *you*? That's where the big challenge comes in; that's the exciting stuff.

Are you in competition with yourself? Or with others? This is the thing in my life that I strive to balance the most. From a negative talk–positive talk perspective, I'm really hard on myself. It's not so much about comparing myself to others; it's about knowing what I *can* do or having a sense for what I think I can do and then struggling with how much I can do to make that happen. I'm really a hard-driving person. I'm the kind of person who from the minute I get up, I'm going until I drop into bed. I have a hard time relaxing. If I watch TV, I'm stretching or folding the clothes. I don't know if I consider myself Type A; I suppose I would be, but I don't consider myself a hyperperson. I have this methodical way of moving through the day, and if there's a moment, then I'm doing something productive. I'm hard on myself, so if I take time down that isn't scheduled, then I go, *You weren't workin' hard enough; you shoulda done that, and therefore you didn't get this done.* That's the voice I fight a lot. Well, I don't want to say I fight it; I try and subdue it because I do believe—and this is probably the one thing in my coaching that I don't practice what I preach—you gotta relax, rest, things like that. I rest in my training; I schedule that in, but I'm definitely pushing myself probably a little too hard, and that can backfire.

The goal with being an athlete is to ride a fine line of being at your top fitness without falling off the fence in the sense of injury, depression, or overtraining. There's this fine line in order to race and be fit enough to race at an elite level. That's sort of the beauty or the challenge of being the top athlete in a fitness-type sport: training hard enough where you're able to race at that level but not falling off. That's really difficult. I fell off a lot, and I learned a lot from falling off the fence. I still fight with that. I still try and figure out what's the balance, what my priorities are.

Right now, that's the thing I'm trying to discover: What are my priorities in reference to sport, in reference to relationships, in reference to career? For the first time in my life, I'm considering the possibility of having a family. Is that something that I want to do? Maybe because my clock's ticking and I haven't figured it out—that's a whole other thing I've thought about, and now I start wondering if that's something I want to do and if it is, I need to figure that out because there's not a whole lot of time left. That's a tough one.

Balance. How do I want to balance? A part of me misses the monofocus of sport, that all-encompassing way of being. You give up a lot in your life to be at that level, but it's really worth it. I'm actually doing a term paper right now on male-dominant sports, and I'm interviewing a lot of people who are in male-dominant sports—basketball, football, baseball, hockey—compared to adventure racing, which is a male-dominant sport for all intents and purposes, but women are on teams so how does that team dynamic change, and how does the perception of the team dynamic change compared to these guys who play with just guys? It's been fascinating. I'm interviewing only elite athletes who play at either intercollegiate or professional levels. It's very interesting to see the differences and similarities.

You know what? It's true: men are from Mars and women from Venus. I had an interview today, and the guy I was talking to brought that up. He said the biggest difference is communication, which is really true. How does he communicate with women on his team? This guy has actually raced with an all-men's team in adventure racing. He says that's really what it comes down to. These guys on the male team are not as good communicators with women as those on the coed teams. I could generalize and say that I've noticed that most of the men who adventure-race on an elite level [with women] have better relationships with women in their personal lives. They would be able to relate to women better.

The other thing that this guy I interviewed today said, "But look at the women who do this sport who are good." He mentioned me and two other women in the United States. He said, "You guys are the kind of girls who hang out with guys. You're kinda guy-girls." Which is really true. I know the other women he was talking about: we train with men, we hang out with men, we know how to talk the guy thing. There's a big difference. Whereas taking a woman who's an athlete in a female realm and putting her on an adventure-racing team, it's a real different thing if she's not used to being around guys; it's a different dynamic. There's some give and take. The guys have feminine qualities, and the women have masculine qualities; that kind of works, kind of comes together.

I asked questions about the qualities of a team player that show respect for other team players. The guys said, "A player who can come to me and ask me questions is showing respect; they're acknowledging that I have something to give them." In adventure racing, the responses have been "a teammate who can ask for help *and* a teammate who can give help." In adventure racing, you look for people who are humble in that "I need to be able to ask for help and be humble in that way to my team." It's not a respect thing for them; they expect me to do it so that I can be good for the team. Whereas these guys are looking for questions to be asked to show respect and loyalty. It's kind of a dominance thing, whereas on the other team, it's more of a function of efficiency in a sense.

Women in their twenties and thirties are less fearful than women in their forties, fifties, sixties. Younger women don't have a cognizance of fear; they haven't been exposed to a lot of fearful things unless they had some kind of abuse situation in their life. Older women have fear, but they also have a maturity about deciding to take on the thing that makes them fearful. I would have to say that the women around my age seem to have the hardest time with taking on fear and then executing it and being able to overcome it. This is a weird age for women—their thirties—because we're coming off the end of the hard-core feminist age, and now feminism is still really strong, but questions have come up about feminism.

Guys are trying to figure out what to do with women. We're relating to men our age who are a little confused, so that makes us a little confused about what we're supposed to be doing. We feel strongly about what we *want* to do, but we still question *what* we want to do. I think those doubts carry over into other parts of our lives. I don't really feel that way so much for me, but I suppose I do from a relationship and family standpoint. But I see that in a lot with women I work with.

Women in their thirties have benefited from the women's movement. It's been really freeing, so now we have choices. You could say that the good news is that we have all these choices, and the bad news is that we have all these choices. You can do whatever you want with your life, but now it's not defined, so we have to figure out what we want to do with our lives. Young women are sort of saying, "Yeah, I can do whatever I want with my life. That's cool." I look at my mother, who's seventy, and she doesn't really understand what I'm doing in my life because everything was defined for her. We have all these choices, and we're not quite sure what to do with them. Some women do better with that than others. I find it to be a positive thing.

I like having choices, but I'm also not a mainstream kind of woman. I haven't gone the regular route—career, getting married, family—although I have been married actually.

He was supportive of my racing. He was a cyclist and was very athletic, but he didn't race professionally. I think there was an issue with that. "I support what you're doing, but when are you gonna quit and start having kids?" I had ideals of marriage. I grew up in a Catholic family, so I had the ideals of the marriage, the kids, and the white picket fence. Then what I realized when I got into the marriage was that it wasn't what I wanted at that time in my life, because I was enjoying being an athlete and successful, making money, and I wanted to do that for as long as I could. I needed to be in an environment that was supportive and allowed me to live that out. I was in my late twenties, early thirties.

Talk about choices, there was a difficult decision because the decision I made to leave the relationship was very selfish. It was about me moving into other realms of my life, moving forward with the career in sport. Again, it wasn't that he wasn't supportive of that *sort of,* but there was still this need to feel that someone was accepting me fully for whatever realm I decided to take on in my life. That was a really difficult thing for me, the most difficult thing in my life—going through divorce. It questioned everything I was brought up with: about marriage and family and commitment, what does marriage mean—all those things I took for granted growing up in a Catholic family. That's kind of what you did. All of a sudden I realized, *Wow, I'm the kind of woman who questions those things. What does that mean? What does that say about me?* I went through a couple of years of really personal evaluation, a lot of therapy, and really looked into what was I really about, what made me fulfilled in my life. I got into another long-term relationship with a man who accepted me for who I was, totally, completely, and unconditionally. That was really a good thing for me. I realized that that was what I wanted to pursue, and what I needed was to be in an environment that was really supportive of that.

Again, we're dealing with the challenge of history and the challenge of the fact that that's the way it's always been. You also can't dispute the fact that women have babies, and the mother, at least when a child is very young, is the one who needs to take care of the kid, for the most part, and so that's a tough thing to get away from. So then you go, *OK, she's gonna have the babies, and so it makes sense for her to stay home and give up her career.* I do know of some men who have done it the other way around, and it's worked out pretty well, but you have to have a man who's willing to do that. We challenge history, and we also challenge our sense of maternalness. You can't really dispute that. I don't know if it's necessarily a bad thing. I definitely consider myself a feminist, but I'm also, in sociological terms, a functionalist who sees that things are the way they are because they're supposed to be that way. Are women minorities? Do we have challenges in our lives that men don't have? Yeah. But it's that way because of history. We're working toward changing that, but it's not going to happen overnight. What I try to do in my life is just live my life as a woman who goes after what she wants and not to let discrimination get in my way. I think I've been able to do it for the most part.

It's easier for me to say because I've been self-employed for a long time now. I'm not in a corporate situation where I'm dealing with men, where I'm dealing with discrimination and sexual harassment and all those other things that can go on. So in one sense, I've had freedom to be able to express and define my career as I've wanted to do it, and I haven't had any limitations from men or whatever on what I do. It's just about me. I think I've been fortunate that way. I don't feel oppression from men, so it's easy for me to feel positive about being a woman. I don't have those angers from past experiences that I think a lot of women carry.

Nature is my religion, my spiritual life. For me to go out running in the woods really connects me to higher things. I like that. I like the beach. I like going kayaking. I think that's what keeps me in Santa Cruz because I look at my career, and the dilemma is I could be doing a lot more if I lived in a bigger area, a bigger city—I could be making more money, there would be more opportunities—so I struggle with that a lot. I think, *What do I want to do? Do I want to stay here and have my little niche and feel comfortable, or do I need to go out and spread my wings a little bit?* I like the attitude here, especially for women. You have a freedom here to do and express yourself the way that you want and feel you need to. That really works for me. But in some ways, I feel sti-fled a little bit. From a relationship perspective, I definitely feel stifled. I don't meet very many men in this area who interest me, and the last two guys I've dated have lived in big cities—not that the big city is the way to go, but it's just a different career drive, to what they're doing in their lives. I need some-one who's proactive that way—going after things. That's tough to find here.

I found I'm a really good alone person. I don't have a problem being alone. I'm very good at entertaining myself. I love to read, go downtown, wander around, go to the movies. And I'm a pretty happy person. But I'm finally at a point in my life where I want companionship. I can be happy alone, but when I'm with someone, everything is enhanced that much more—sharing the day-to-day things and sharing what's going on in my life, having discussions, having that connection with another person. I would like that again at some point.

It's not that I want to have kids right now, but I know that if I don't do it, I'll regret it when I'm fifty. The other thing that's tough is that I don't want to do it solo. To me, having children is about having it with a partner; that's important to me. If I don't end up with another person who has that same goal, then I'll accept that it didn't happen. I'm in a relationship now and we're trying to decide if we want to check that out. It's a tough call. I also got out of a relationship about a year and a half ago, but we were really con-nected—we still are in our lives. This person is still my best friend basically, so that's tough. I look a lot at that, and I question. He doesn't know if he wants to have kids, so again if I decide I want to have children, this person is out of the question. It's tough. Relationship dilemmas. I'm trying not to get really wrapped up in it and let it bum me out, because it's not all smoothed out. Then I realized it's all just life—good learning experiences. I feel really grateful that I have these people in my life; a lot of people don't. I feel thank-ful for both of them being in my life the way they are, those wonderful, warm relationships. It's nice. However it's going to happen, I don't know. Roll the dice. Your guess is as good as mine at this point.

I don't necessarily need one day a week off. I've done this for so long, so I schedule a rest day—it's kind of a spontaneous thing if I think I need it.

I know when I've pushed a little too hard, and I'm really hard core about getting enough sleep. Making sure people get enough sleep is superimportant. Sleep is a time when we recharge our batteries, and if we don't do it, then we're working on less-than. I sleep only seven or eight hours and need that to function properly. My days change a lot, and I like that. I don't have the nine-to-five. If I want to take a whole day and train, I'll do it.

I plan my week the way I plan my clients' week. I evaluate the week I just did, the way I do for my clients; then I plan my week of training. I pretty much stick with it unless I get into the week and things aren't feeling right. Everyone has entire weeks when it's just not happening, and you're dragging yourself through every workout. Those are the weeks where I'll take a week off. On Thursday, I'm supposed to do two hours of training but I'll go, *You know what? I need to take the day off, need to rest.*

It's definitely planned and structured just like everybody else. In order to reach goals in life, you have to have a plan. I suppose you could reach them, but you're not going to get there as quickly and efficiently as if you have a plan. Training is the same way. You can do it haphazardly, but you're not going to reach your goals as efficiently or as quickly or as safely as you potentially could if you have a plan.


I define success as happiness. I think everyone has to define happiness for themselves. For myself, it's liking myself—feeling good about what I've done and what I'm doing in my life. That doesn't mean it has to be 100 percent of the time, 24–7. It's about having a general sense that I feel good about myself as a person, a woman, that I'm accepting of who I am. That's a really tough thing. To me that's the ultimate. If we can accept ourselves, then everything else will kind of fall into place. So happiness to me is success. If you feel a contentment with your life—and contentment doesn't mean resting on your laurels—it just means that you can look back and go, *Yeah, I really screwed up, but look at how much I learned.* Or, *What a neat thing, a positive that was for me!* and be able to accept whatever it is that happens. Part of that is learning not to make as many mistakes. We have to work hard to understand ourselves, so a lot of it is about doing the work. Doing the work. You can bitch and moan about your life, and that's OK if you're doing the work. If you're not doing the work, then it's difficult to get to a place where you're accepting, because there's always doubt, there's always wonder, and there's always fear.

I think human beings are driven and motivated by fear. That's a really out-of-control place to be. A scary place to be. Fear perpetuates fear. I've never really been like that, but I've seen a lot of other people be that way. I think if we could learn how to accept—even if it's accepting that you're fearful—that's OK. It's accepting our shortcomings. I think the acceptance gives you confidence, and the acceptance *is* confidence. I don't know if it would be the opposite of. It's like knowing how much you can do and being honest about that—not being what you would define as lazy or doing less than you think you can do, but striving at a pace that feels good for you: challenged and yet still comfortable and safe, and not backing down from your beliefs but learning what those beliefs are and what they mean. It's tough being a human being, and it's a lot of work. Sometimes it's tiring, and I think finding that balance is my biggest challenge. Sometimes I feel that I'm tired of working hard on myself all the time, but I'm always analyzing myself and looking at this and how I could do it better, and reading books, and talking to people. Where does it end?

I'm very goal oriented; I plan this and that. But for some reason I have never been one of those people who says, "This is where I want to be in five years." I suppose that's the spontaneous part of me, which is why I take each year and decide what I want to accomplish for the year. I set goals around that particular year. It strikes me as odd that I don't plan far ahead, because I'm that way in everything else in my life, but if you look at my year, it's pretty much planned. But next year, I have no idea. At this point in my life, maybe I'll move to New York and have children. Or maybe I'll be single and not have any kids and end up doing the same thing. I haven't a clue.

I've prided myself on doing the things I've done in my life. I have a lot of nieces and nephews, and I'm very close to my brothers and sisters and their families. I coach a lot of women who have children. I realize how challenging that is—to have children. A part of me is afraid to do it. I think I would be a good parent, but to have this being that's 100 percent, twenty-four hours a day relying on me—that's a scary thing for me. I wonder, Do I want to take that on? Do I want to be that way? I've been so selfish with my life. To have a career and be successful in sport, you have to be selfish. That's just the way it goes. Any elite athlete is a very selfish person.

I don't consider *selfish* as having a negative connotation. With the women I coach—I have to come up with a different word—allow this "thing" in your life to let you be selfish. Grab hold of it for you. I think I've grabbed hold of my life for *me*. It doesn't mean I haven't been nurturing to my family or relationships, but my career has been my priority and what I've wanted to accomplish. In a family, that shifts. I wonder if I would be able to do it and feel good about it and still feel fulfilled, still feel intellectually stimulated, still feel all those things that I like to feel. I have fear. I have questions around how I would feel being in that realm, especially if I were in a relationship where the man was the breadwinner and I stayed home with the kids. How would I feel about that? It's a really tough one for me. I don't know. I think I would have a difficult time with it. Maybe I wouldn't, though, because I would be in the realm of the challenge of raising children, and I would realize how all-encompassing that was.

Adventure racing is really challenging, beyond what anyone could ever possibly imagine anything in their life. I wonder, if I do this mainstream thing in my life like having kids, will I miss the fight? Will I miss being in the hunt, miss the challenge of getting down and dirty with the guys for five days? That's kind of what I wonder.

In terms of my physical body, I feel strong now. I feel healthy. I think that's part of why I take it year to year, because a lot of it is about a physical assessment: How do I feel? How many races do I want to do next year given how I feel? So far, I'd have to say I don't really feel that different. I'm not as fast as I used to be in my early thirties. That seems to be the first thing to go. Physiologically, things do change. You tend to lose that speed element; it's pretty common. I also haven't trained for speed, because I'm doing longer distances.

Recovery from really tough workouts is a little bit longer than it used to be, but other than that, from an endurance standpoint, it may be better than it's ever been—psychologically better than it's ever been. I think that comes with maturity. But endurance is also about mental toughness. A lot of ultrarunners, for instance, are in their late thirties, early forties, because it's about being able to be in your head and hold pace and really tough it out. Same in adventure racing. Most folks are about my age. I'd probably be considered middle-aged for an adventure racer, right in the middle of the peak. It's all about desire: how long do I want to do it? If you can't make yourself go out and train at that level every day, then it's not gonna happen. That's the shift. It's not so much whether my body can do it, unless I have some injury or something that takes me out; it's more about how long I desire to continue.

It's a lot of work. Being a professional athlete has been put out as a really glamorous thing, but there's a lot of gut wrenching. When you look at the Olympics, for instance, all of those athletes worked their asses off every day of their lives for the last ten years probably, in a completely nonromantic situation. We romanticize being in the Olympics. Those people are hard workers; they have talent, and they're hard workers. That's why they're at that level. It's not because some angel came down and granted them some divine whatever so they could go to the Olympics; it's all that hard work. That's what the public doesn't see. Even people I trained with when I was a professional triathlete, that was my job, and a lot of people didn't take it seriously. It was like, Terry gets to train and how fun that is. It *is* fun, but it's a lot of work and there's a lot of pressure. If it's pouring rain, I gotta get on my bike. It's not as if I can opt to sit home and read the paper on Sunday. It's about everyday consistency. In order to be a better athlete, that's what it takes. That's what I stress with my clients. It's not, *I'm going to train for a week, then take a couple of weeks off, then I might come back and do a few things, then I'm going to* . . . If you want to get fit, you gotta be consistent, week after week after week, as much as your life can allow. That's where you see results. Just like losing weight, it doesn't happen overnight. We want a quick fix; everyone wants it to be fast. We want it to be ugly free, and we want everything to be wonderful. It doesn't work that way.

People assume because of all my working out that I haven't had any kind of weight or self-image problem. That's not true at all. Do you know a woman who doesn't have a self-image problem? Absolutely not. That's part of the acceptance thing. Again, it's about accepting that those are issues. I don't have the typical triathlete's body. I'm stocky, so I'm big for my sport—big for endurance sports. A lot of people look at me and say, "Oh, you're a sprinter," because I'm powerful looking. But I'm not a sprinter. I enjoy endurance sports; that's what I've chosen to do in my life. So a lot of my insecurities have come around not having the typical body and having to deal with my perceptions of what's OK around that. I've never had eating disorders or anything like that, but I definitely struggled with wanting to be smaller and not being able to accept the fact that if I work out, I get big muscles; I have big bones, so I tend to carry the big muscles. That's kind of the way it goes. I'm also not the kind of woman who can eat anything I want and not put weight on. I probably eat more than most other people, but if I start piggin' out . . . As you get older, even though I'm training, it's a lot of work to take those extra pounds off.

It's about finally, one day, looking in the mirror and saying, "This is the body I have. I'm not going to have her body, and I'm never going to have her body, and I'm never going to have long legs." That's the way it goes. I make all these choices. I can either bum myself out all the time and wish I had something else going on, or I can just go, *What a strong, wonderful body I have.* I'm not petite and muscular; I'm big and muscular. Look at all these things that I can do with my body. Every woman could say that about herself.

We all have things about our body that are unique to us and that are beautiful to us. We need to zone in on those. I can hang with the best of them in just about anything. I can go out and do adventure races, and my body is very tough and resilient, and I can beat the shit out of myself and I'm still going to hold up. It's amazing. I've had injuries, but for the amount of abuse I give to myself, it's amazing how much my body's held up. I've learned to love my strength and love the fact that I'm a big, strong woman. That's a difference now versus when I was younger. I think that's a place to strive for: accepting who you are, knowing the body you have has limitations. We need to accept those, *but* there are so many things you can do with that.

I come from the premise that human beings are really good people. What we need to do is learn how to let that shine. We all have it in us. I coach that way. Everyone's an athlete, and all I need to do is facilitate that aspect of them to come out and shine. We're all beautiful people, and we're all physically wonderful, and it's just about letting those things shine and come out—and accept the good things and not be so hard on yourself all the time. It's really tough.

When an athlete has an injury, I sit down with that person and say, "Let's explore all the potential things you can do to make injury better." If you're doing all those things, there's nothing else you can do. You have this body, and you're doing everything you can or are physically able to do to be fitter, to lose weight, and whatever else it is that you're trying to accomplish. If you're honest about that and about that process, then accept the situation because you don't have control over anything else. All you can do is what you can control. People forget there's a lot we can control, a lot we can control about what happens in our head, about what happens physically, about what happens in our lives. It's pretty amazing, actually. We make choices. We look at our options, and then we make choices. If you're honest about doing that, then get on with it. I have a lot of tough love around that. I see so many people just wallowing.

Find what it takes in your life to accept yourself and therefore be happy with what you have. If that means taking on new things, then find a way to do it. If that means hiring a professional, if that means reading a book, if that means learning how to communicate about going to therapy—whatever it takes. Just because we're adults doesn't mean we have the tools to be in good relationships and to have great careers to make a lot of money and be skinny. It doesn't really work that way. A lot of times we have to gather tools to put in our toolbox. So gather the tools in whatever way you need to make that happen, so that the bottom line is that you can look in the mirror and go, "I really love this woman I'm looking at. Look how beautiful she is. Look at what a wonderful person she is." If you can do that, then life will be a happy place. Definitely.

*The most important lesson that I learned or am still learning is to let go. Let go of situations and people who are not nurturing to my spirit, my mind, and body. Let go of the past—people I loved who no longer love me the same way or the way I was used to being loved. To see that some people and situations I thought were for my highest and best good are really not. To look beyond the delusion of the outward senses and see what is truly important.*

KAMALA DEOSARANSINGH

# Kamala Deosaransingh

## PROFILE

I met Kamala Deosaransingh at a book signing I did for my book about women in their seventies. Even though only in her thirties, she came because her mother was turning seventy, and, as she says, "My mother is one of my best friends. I am very blessed with such a positive role model. She is not perfect, but her desire to be the best is inspiring." Kamala realizes how vastly her thirties differed from the thirties her mother experienced. Her mother was married and had five children by the time she was thirty-eight, Kamala's age.

Not all younger women are aware of how the women's movement affected their lives, but Kamala recognizes that "the women's movement shaped my life. Gloria Steinem was a role model for me in terms of believing that a woman could be anything she wanted career-wise, if she really wanted it."

Perhaps one of the most pressing matters for Kamala is her desire for a husband, children, and a home. She spoke eloquently for many women of an entire generation who feel that their opportunity to have biological children may be passing them by.

## Finding Her Heart

I grew up as the youngest child in an upper-middle-class family of immigrant parents—well, my father was an immigrant from Trinidad, and my mother was first-generation Mexican. I did not really realize my parents were upper middle class until I went to high school and the boys who were interested in me came to my house, and I went to their houses, and we compared notes. My parents are very unmaterialistic people and valued education, integrity, and ethics more than anything else. I was a straight A student until I got to high school and rebelled against my parents for pressuring me to "perform." I went from a straight A student to getting Ds and Fs. I was mad.

I look back at this period of time with much compassion for my entire family and realize that unresolved anger and pain from childhood can cause much hurt for all concerned. I made it through high school and into community college and then into the University of California system. I wanted to be a writer, but knew that I couldn't make a living at it. I also had a great desire to help people. My father was a role model for this. He had a strong desire to help the people in his village in Trinidad and as a result became a doctor. He eventually went back with my mother, who is a nurse, to serve the people in the village he grew up in.

A dream that I entertained for some time, and still do, is to be a child psychologist. I wanted to help kids in some way. However, ironically I sit in front of a computer all day and analyze data and have no contact with children. I help them indirectly because I work on studies that try to find the causes of birth defects. A worthy cause. I like the research process, but find the lack of direct contact with people, coupled with the pettiness of office politics, unfulfilling at times. I think about moving my career into a different direction within the health care arena.

The images that stretched my imagination as a child were from books. I loved to read. I read when I got home from school, after homework, during meals if possible. And if I was reading an especially good story, I would prop a book on the ledge outside the shower door and read in the shower! (Kids do strange things.) The stories of young women living everyday lives and their thoughts and feelings touched me.

When I went to junior high, I felt different than I had felt in grammar school. I started to feel a distancing from my group of school friends. They were nice, but I started to feel different and spent more time alone. I think it was the basic angst of coming of age. Then in high school I got a boyfriend, and my sexuality opened up. It was opening up before I got a boyfriend, but then he came along and pushed the door.

Meeting Chris and his introducing me to meditation and other ways to use my mind constructively has been the important thing during my lifetime. Chris was a big part of my life. We were opposites in some ways but very much kindred spirits. He and his family were my family when I was having problems with my own family. They thought I was great. Chris's dad is a psychologist and had a strong interest in alternative medicine, meditation, and Eastern thought and religion. When I was leaving their house, he would give me a big hug. This meant a lot to me at that time. Chris and his father and I are still in touch with each other. I make sure of it. They were a big part of my life.

Through meditation practice, I have come to know myself better and feel more comfortable with myself. This inward exploration has been worthwhile; I have come to realize better the reasons why we are here: to give and receive love. Pretty basic. I have come to appreciate life more and realize that it is precious and tenuous. Life and time are not something to take for granted. They are truly a gift.

The women's movement shaped my life. Gloria Steinem was a role model for me in terms of believing that a woman can be anything she wants careerwise, if she really wants it. I think that the newer generation doesn't really know what the women's movement was all about. They are reaping the benefits of it, but like eight-track decks, it may just be history to them.

I met Gloria Steinem in person at the local community college that I attended when I was eighteen. I remember her being a woman who had such a vision for what women could be beyond what societal mores were dictating for them. She reinforced in me that women do not need men to be complete and, to quote her, "that women are becoming the men they wanted to marry." She has been such a spokeswoman in aiding the repression and outdated ways society saw women. I like her because she is soft-spoken and has quiet grace. She is a woman with a vision for the future of women in American society.

My parents both came from very poor backgrounds, and through their desire to better themselves and be a helping force in their communities and the world, they became educated. Despite the fact that my father's parents were illiterate and very poor, my father had a strong desire to become a doctor and help the poor in his village. He attained this goal by overcoming many economic and emotional barriers as well as racial discrimination in this country. He does not have the word *impossible* in his vocabulary. He believes that if you want anything badly enough and are willing to make the necessary sacrifices, it is not beyond your reach. I have never heard my parents feel sorry about their lot in life; they have always looked ahead to see ways to get around the challenges that face them. I think that is one of the greatest lessons I learned from them: to look ahead for ways to get around an obstacle instead of just complaining about it. Use your mental faculties creatively to navigate through life's difficulties.

My mother always stressed for her daughters to have careers and not depend on anyone to support or help them. She herself had a career, while my friends' mothers did not. She raised five kids by herself because my father was always working. She maintains herself by doing regular exercises, and she's always reading about new ways to do things or look at things. She laughs and loves her grandchildren a lot. She believes that the utmost thing in marriage is commitment, and her commitment shows in the way she is concerned about our lives. My mother is one of my best friends. She is not perfect, but her desire to be the best is inspiring.

What I love most is to have good friends and family around me—to spend time and do things that are fun to do together. What displeases me the most is when family and friends disappointment me.

The greatest happiness in my life has been my friends and family that I have shared time with. The greatest sorrow has been the ending of some of these relationships or the change of some of these relationships to a different form, the letting go of old relationships.

My advice to women who have visions or passions and want to pursue them is to go for it. Don't listen to people when they talk negatively about your dreams. They are not you. Life is short, and people come and go in your life, but you are always left with yourself. Live life abundantly!!! Go for it!

My lifestyle is a quiet one. I sometimes wonder why I choose to spend so much time by myself, but I do. I always had close friends when I was younger and was popular in school, but I like to spend my time with one or two close friends and my family. I get up in the morning and meditate and then go to work. Lately, I have been trying to get up early so I can read parts of a meditation book or read a couple of pages on investing and finances. When I get home, I eat, maybe exercise, talk on the phone. I have just a couple of close friends, but I seem to be always busy.

I wish I had more close friends, but I am very grateful for my friend, Frank. Although I have moved away and have been living in northern California, my friendship with Frank has become closer and more intimate. I really think it is because we are both into self-growth. He meditates, and the feeling is mutual about our friendship. I have another close friend, Louis. Frank, Louis, and I are all close friends, and we are all grateful for the presence of our friendship in each other's lives. Frank, Louis, and I have spent many memorable times together and have laughed a lot. We have seen each other go through "firsts" in our lives and laughed and cried together.

I find myself trying to define what I want in my life. There is a place or time for romantic love in my life, but I am not very proactive about attaining it. I need to go out more and mingle, but I find that it doesn't come easily for me to socialize with new people. I know that I will find the love of my life someday, because I know I have a lot to share with someone else. It is just finding that someone. I feel that is the most important decision a woman makes in her life. A man can be your greatest blessing or your greatest torment.

My fantasy about aging is that I will age gracefully, which means that I will keep active physically and mentally. That I will be this beautiful wise old woman who is open-hearted and open-minded to the people and situations around her. That I will not grow old but keep flexible in the mind and body. That I will have a rich life of family and friends. That I will some way find the center of who I am and in so doing that I find the love of my life. I think they go hand in hand in some way—finding your true nature as well as finding your true love. I was told by a wise Buddhist priest that even if you find your love at your last breath, that would be fine.

The negative aspect about aging is that you become less desirable and less valuable as an aging woman in American society. This is a great challenge American women have to deal with. We live in a society that is conditioned to value youth in their women as a sign of beauty and desirability. As a woman in her late thirties who is not married, I find myself a bit fearful about my future, about my place in this society. What is my place? Where is my place? The positive aspect of aging is that you become wiser and more in touch with your true nature if you are into self-growth and self-knowledge. These gifts that you work for internally may not be apparent externally until you really get to know someone.

My mother is a role model of an older woman who comes to mind. She exercises every day, which keeps her body limber and her mind sharp. She keeps the house maintained and in working order. The single thing I most admire about my mom is her strength and resolve in the midst of adverse family situations. She fought hard to maintain a family when the family was going through extreme problems. She sought out therapy and read a lot of books to help her understand what the problem was and how to work with it. I wish I could have half the strength my mother has, yet I may not need such strength in my life, because my path, I feel, will not require that type of strength.

To nurture myself, I get on the phone and talk to my close friends. I take a long walk on a summer day. I meditate. I get a facial. I take a shower. If I were still living by the beach, I would take a long walk on the beach. I feel most alive when I am outside, walking in the hills—when the wind blows through my hair, when I smell the jasmine outside. When I am making love to the man I love and he loves me back. Having a long conversation with my girlfriends about our lives.

The most important lesson that I learned or am still learning is to let go. Let go of situations and people who are not nurturing to my spirit, my mind, and body. Let go of the past—people I loved who no longer love me the same way or the way I was used to being loved. To see that some people and situations I thought were for my highest and best good are really not. To look beyond the delusion of the outward senses and see what is truly important.

My definition of success is finding your heart or vitality and expressing it. To come from your heart in your life and not being afraid to speak the truth through your actions and words. Success is opening your heart up to your life and dreams, to give and to receive love freely. The one thing that I would love to do in my life is to be a wife and mother; to be in a committed intimate relationship with a man I am totally in love with and I respect and who is my best friend. This relationship would lead to having my own family, a home, and a beautiful garden.

I know some women get depressed on their thirtieth birthday, but I remember clearly that I didn't. My mother and I probably went to the theater in Los Angeles and then out to dinner. I looked forward to my thirties, and they have gone by really fast.

On my thirty-eighth birthday, I went to southern California to visit my parents. My friend, Lalitha, and her mother and brother were coming for dinner. Lalitha is a good friend who is from India, and I wanted her to meet my parents. I thought it would be just an uneventful dinner, but I forgot that

my parents do not do birthday dinners in an ordinary way. They went outside and started the barbecue and were going to barbecue chicken. They put
a nice tablecloth on the dining room table and put the china out. They had
bought champagne and a birthday cake. Lalitha came over and brought me
a dozen long-stemmed red roses. I was touched. Nobody had given me a
dozen roses in my life. It was meaningful because Lalitha has been a good
friend this past year. My sister came over and also brought me some presents.

Later in the evening, my sister and I were at the table, and I told her
that this was one birthday where I found myself depressed. My biological
clock seemed to be ticking louder, and time seemed to be passing, with no
prospects of having a child. I forget to remind myself, though, that it has
been only in the past year and a half that I really wanted to have children.
My sister, who is divorced and has two children, said that all children are the
world's children. I always remind myself that I can adopt children if I can't
have them.

What is significant regarding my thirties is that I have not suffered from
the angst of who am I. I have been more concerned in establishing some
sort of career path for myself, becoming self-sufficient and self-reliant emotionally and financially. Sometimes I ask myself why is this important to me,
and my answer is that the more self-reliant I am, the more able I will be to
help others.

My thirties differed enormously from the thirties my mother experienced. My mother was married and had five children by the time she was
my age. She was very much committed to raising her children and being a
wife. She did not have the opportunities that I had growing up, and tradition and the social culture at the time were different for her.


The last time I surprised myself was when the man I was seeing (only for a
brief time) told me that he was also seeing someone else. I felt hurt, mad,
and angry, but at the same time I had a certain amount of detachment that
I did not have before. I did not completely freak. I realized that people will
do what they will and I have little control over their actions. I can control
only what I feel and what I do. I also have learned that you cannot make

someone love you; you can only be who you are. (I am still trying to practice this one.) I also realized that I just need to give the love I have and try to expect nothing in return (without being masochistic, that is).

My relationship with my body is OK. I used to pay more attention to how it looked and felt. Then the stress of some jobs I had made me neglect it, and I gained about twelve pounds. Now I try to take a walk almost every day. I still need to eat more fruits and vegetables. I realize I cannot look like I did when I was twenty-two, and I accept it. Women can heal their self-image by finding their inner beauty and loving themselves more by appreciating their soulful qualities.

My spiritual practice consists of meditating at least once a day. I read spiritual books, and I take walks outside, in nature. I try to treat people the way I want to be treated. I try to be kind and practice the three R's: right meditation, right thought, and right action. I try to remember that life is short and to laugh, have fun, and be kind.

I look forward in the next decade to having more freedom of expressing who I really am, not what I thought people wanted me to be—to be able to give and receive love more freely and to open my heart up to life and love, to laugh more—until it hurts.

*I spent my twenties looking for answers, and only when I turned thirty did I realize there weren't any, and that I was asking the wrong question. Instead of asking, "What is the answer?" I should have asked, "Why or how can this be meaningful?"*

KATHERINE SPILDE

# Katherine Spilde

## PROFILE

Katherine Spilde was born in Moorhead, Minnesota, in 1968. She grew up in a very rural small town in Minnesota, with a population of about a thousand. The town is on an Indian reservation, a fact that became important in our conversation as Katherine and I spoke about the unfolding of her life. She says that while growing up, she was aware that "there was a big world out there that I wasn't part of, but I was not sure if I would ever be allowed to be a part of it."

After moving several times and attending various universities, Katherine settled in Santa Cruz, and she eventually received a Ph.D. in anthropology. As inveterate readers of the *New York Times,* we met one Sunday morning at our local market where we were both buying the paper. Who knew, we would joke with each other after we became close friends, that we would meet in Aptos, the sweet little seaside community where there is endless beauty?

It turned out that we lived only two blocks from each other. During our many two-hour-long beach walks, we shared our life stories and dreams for our future. Katherine told me the many challenges she had faced in life: repeated eating disorders, alcoholism, and the death of her brother. But her accomplishments in her personal and professional lives have happily triumphed.

# Finding Meaning

At the time I was growing up, in the town itself (of the entire reservation) probably one-quarter of the people are non-Indian. Of those non-Indians, almost all of them live in this town because that's where the school is, that's where the county government is, and most of the non-Indians who live there are teachers and business owners. There was only one high school when I was growing up there, so all of us went to the same school. At the time, I didn't think anything about integration, until I went away and realized what that meant. Again, I think that was a piece of my eventually moving to Minneapolis: interacting with a lot more white people and hearing their views about Native peoples, figuring out how reservations fit into the bigger America, and that it was a marginalized place, and why so many people were unemployed. I ended up asking really different questions and also seeking new answers to things that I hadn't thought to ask about. Why do both of my parents have a job and neither of my friends' parents have a job—and they're Native? The unemployment rate was 85 percent. It was one of the highest unemployment rates in the nation. The county, located entirely within the reservation, consistently had the lowest standard of living in the state. Yet both of my parents had jobs. I wasn't sophisticated enough as a high school student or young person to understand that. When I moved away and started college is when I really started seeing myself in the world.

The other big thing about moving away was that I got to go to the movies. Where we lived was a good hour and a half from Fargo, North Dakota, which was the big town, so it was a big deal to go there—to go shopping and go to the movies. That was something I really longed for. We didn't have cable TV. I had this yearning; I knew there was more, and I wanted it. I wanted to be not just looking at but participating in the world. Minneapolis was my entree into that, yet that didn't seem like enough either. I was there only one year, and that was when I met my best friend, the first person I felt ever really saw me. She was a go-getter, and she was moving to Spain. I had never known anyone who had moved out of the state of Minnesota, let alone to Spain. I just thought, Who is this woman? I want to be like her.

I was really scared to stay without her at school; she was my best friend. I was very shy, and it was only through her that I had a social life. But I didn't speak any languages, so I couldn't do the Europe thing. I found this national program where you could go to another school within the United States, so I chose the University of Hawaii. That is a huge marker for me: going out of the state to a place with no winter. This is how I've learned to think about it: I feel like I grew up in a place where people find themselves and don't feel like they had a lot of choice in where they're living, whether it's farmers who have children and generations after generations stay and work the land—not deliberately choosing to live there, but just being born into this location. Of course, the same is true for Native people who find themselves on a reservation. Think about the history of being placed there. In Hawaii, I felt that everyone I met who was living there had moved there on purpose. It was a really different sense. I didn't know a lot of Native people there, just a few in school. In terms of the tourists and the general feeling in the air, the idea that everyone who was there wanted to be there, including me—I didn't feel like I just woke up one day and someone had put me there—gave me a sense of agency in my own life.

If you're around other people who are doing what they want to do, it changes your whole environment. I learned so much about the world in Hawaii; that's where I discovered anthropology, where I decided I could participate in the world. When I was a bartender, I met people from all over the world: Australia, New Zealand, all the Pacific islands, and Japan. It was unbelievable to me. I really blossomed and felt a new sense of myself as a social person. I could really talk to people.

After I finished college in Hawaii, I moved to Washington, D.C., for graduate school. Living in Washington, living in an urban area, was another major marker for me. Certainly Honolulu is a city, but I was involved in only the tropical, tourist part of the city. I was very free-spirited, went to the beach but didn't interact with the urban part of the island. That part didn't interest me at all. So Washington was my first taste of a real city and politics. My school was four blocks from the White House. The *Washington Post* is your home-town paper. Things are happening in the building next door.

Washington grounded me even more in the world; it helped me to feel that I was a part of something, that I wasn't just watching things. Those years were also incredible. One of the things that was startling about Washington was that because it is a big city, there was a lot of crime. Every day the *Post* would have stories about people being killed. During the crack epidemic, between 1991 and 1993, people were dying over sneakers, over five dollars. I was shocked. After living there a while, I think people become less shocked and maybe just skip over the articles, but it was very shocking to me.

I naively decided I would find out what was going on. It started as a paper for methodology class in anthropology, on how to do fieldwork. You had to choose a community within the city. I decided to do a study of drug dealers. It ended up as the basis for my master's thesis. It really changed my relationship with the city because I began interviewing and hanging out with people who sold drugs on the streets and the prostitutes and trying to get a feeling for what was happening. It just seemed unbelievable to me.

After I started meeting all these people, I became really invested in the issue: in homelessness, prostitution, the street life I had never understood. One of the luxuries of a small town is that I know eight hundred people who would take me in. I'd hate to move back, but the point is that I have a huge safety net. I'd never considered that there would be people on the street for whom there was not one person they could call on for a meal or a place to live. That was really a startling moment for me, and I wanted to talk to them and find out how that could happen.

After I finished my degree, I defied the odds. A lot of people were discouraging me from doing that kind of research, saying, "It's not marketable. How are you possibly going to get a job with this kind of degree?" Well, wouldn't you know, I ended up with a paid position in New York City interviewing drug dealers—possibly the only paid position doing that in the country. A New York research firm gets federal funds to do a host of projects, and one was studying the distribution of drugs in Brooklyn. They needed people who understood ethnographic methods, knew how to talk to the people and interview them, and also how to write about it in a meaningful way.

Living in New York City was the pinnacle of engaging with the world. Every day I would wake up and walk out of my building and say, "These people are New Yorkers; I'm living among New Yorkers." I've always been very aware of where I come from. I would wake up and think, I've made it as far from the reservation as I could go. I'm living in Manhattan now. At that time, that was very important to me—to feel as if I had really washed myself of the place, like I'd sort of caught up with the rest of the world. I knew how to dress; I knew how to interact with people; I had an education; I could support myself; I caught up. I'd always thought I was a little behind socially and culturally because of where I'd lived. I felt as if I'd finally made it, that no one could look at me and tell that I was from a small town in the Midwest.

And yet I felt there was a need to complete my degree all the way. I had the master's degree, but I also knew I had to go all the way. I was doing a lot of work and writing in the research firm but not getting much credit for it because I didn't have a Ph.D. And that's how I ended up in Santa Cruz. Of course, the Santa Cruz years were huge—not just being in Santa Cruz but when doing my research in Minnesota. I moved back to live and do research on the Native American casino there. I finally quit trying to deny where I was from and actually embraced it. It's because of Minnesota that I ended up in New York. It's because of this place that I'm interested in what I'm interested in, that I was probably driven to success because I had something to prove. That was an incredible emotional shift for me. I felt very grateful also that it wasn't simply an emotional journey, like my bowing out of life to go home and have this epiphany. I was able to incorporate it into my research. I was there doing legitimate work while also having these personal revelations.

I felt great that I had discovered anthropology and found a way to merge that with my own questions. My personal questions could be answered at the same time that I was working on legitimate social questions and see how my trajectories sort of intersected with the bigger questions of privilege and what it means to be white, what it means to be Native, why I was the one to get the Ph.D. and not my Native American friends. That was the biggest piece for that year: integrating the part that I had been running from and really feeling that it's something that now I claim rather than deny.

What I've just given you is the sanitized résumé version of my life. There are a number of substories happening in terms of other substrands of my identity: certainly my relationship with my body, my relationship with alcohol, a lot of family issues.

For me it started in adolescence. I wasn't sophisticated enough to articulate my feelings of not being good enough or missing out on the world. I needed to measure my worth against other people in the way that I had learned to do through family and magazines and all the other sources that we get our information from. I ended up becoming really obsessed with my weight and my body. I used my body to explain outside things. For example, my dad left our family when I was twelve. I wasn't sophisticated enough to explain how that could happen, so I decided it was because I was fat. As an adult looking back at that, it was a way to try to make sense of the world. If somebody didn't like me, it was because I was ugly. Everything could be explained through me. I don't think it was because I was narcissistic; it was because I was scared of the unpredictability of adults. I didn't know how I fit into the world, and I needed some mechanism to make sense of things. So I chose my body and what I understood to be my ugliness at the time. That manifested itself in some painful and long-term ways. I became anorexic and got very ill—just sort of bowed out of the world for awhile. I decided that the universe was going to consist of me and what I ate. I was going to shrink it down to the bare essentials, because that's all I could tolerate.

I would go days without eating, and then I got really ill. Certainly I did come to a point where I realized I wasn't running this show anymore. That's one of the really seductive things about anorexia, I think—that you feel special. It's a way to feel better than other people because other people need to eat—and you don't. You've risen to a spiritual level where you can live without food.

All the women in my life were obsessed by food. They would lose weight and then gain it back. Well, I lost weight, and I wasn't going to stop. I had mastered my body. At least that was what I thought. I remember exactly the day, because it was probably the scariest day of my life up until that point. I had gone to the doctor; my mom had made me go to see if I had anything physically wrong with me. She was just freaking out. That was another function of anorexia: my body displayed the problems that were happening. My mother was trying to keep the facade that everything was OK in our family, but how could she continue that story when her daughter was dying in front of everybody's eyes? It's a very visual illness. At the lowest, I weighed about 105 or 110 and was 5'10" at the time. I was very, very ill looking, although my face didn't look that bad.

Looking at pictures now, I'm shocked. People who see these photos don't believe it's me. There's nothing of me there. My eyes, my face, my hair—they don't look like me. For me to look at the photos is strange as well. I don't see myself there either. My mom made me go to the doctor, and they were taking blood from me and I fainted. I woke up and felt for the first time that I came into my body and realized that I felt incredibly vulnerable. I went home and cried and cried and stayed in bed, and that was when I realized I actually wasn't this supreme wonderwoman, control person. Actually this thing had controlled me. It sounds very logical, but it was an incredibly scary feeling since I had created this world where I was running things—and to realize that I wasn't was just unbearable. I also remember thinking I was going to have to kill myself because it was just too unbearable, and I was afraid I was going to die.

But then I decided that if I was to kill myself anyway, I should eat all the food that I liked first. You might as well have a little fun. Eat for a week and then kill myself. I started eating, and I didn't stop. My will to kill myself left; even though I became very miserable, the actual suicidal thoughts left. But I basically gained a hundred pounds in nine months. I went from looking really ill to looking really overweight. It was another painful experience, because again I was expressing the pain to the world. Everyone could look at me and see that something was terribly wrong. There's something about being really thin where people want to help you and nurture you, but when you become fat, you are embodying everything that people despise, so they actually shun you instead of comforting you. All of a sudden there was a shift from, "There's something wrong in that *family*" to "There's something wrong with *her.*" All of a sudden my mother was off the hook. That kept me eating more. When I was starving to death, people could blame her. But when I was now two-hundred-plus pounds, I was just a glutton. There was just something wrong with *me.* I really believed that for awhile; that's how the society views people who eat a lot. There's some deficit.

Then I did what many anorexic people do: I became bulimic. I started throwing up, and I did that for years. When I started, I lost about forty pounds and leveled out at 170, 180. I was very active at the time in my junior year in high school. Then during my senior year, I became really bulimic. I moved away to college and was still bulimic. Things got a little better in Hawaii, but those behaviors manifested themselves in new ways.

I got to Hawaii pretty much a mess emotionally, and all of a sudden people started treating me really differently. People didn't think I was ugly. A lot of men were attracted to me. It was amazing. How can this be? I'm exactly the same. I don't think I handled it very well. I guess I was just so thrilled to have that kind of attention that I didn't want to say no to anybody. I ended up dating a lot, drinking a lot. I don't think it was too unhealthy at the time. Certainly I drank a lot, but so was everybody else; we were in a tourist capital of the United States.

When I got to Washington, D.C., and started graduate school, I decided I wanted to be thin. Looking back and knowing what I know now about eating disorders, I believe that I was just very insecure about graduate school. Was I smart enough? It was a private school—George Washington University. I had come from Hawaii, free-wheelin' and fun. There was this seriousness; my colleagues had gone to schools like Emory and Boston University, and I was scared that I was just this goofball. I joined Weight Watchers in Washington and started strictly limiting my food intake. Then I also adapted to a very strict exercise regimen. That was the way for me to try to control things. All the other stuff was just too scary. So again I had to simplify my life down to the basics, which was just me and food. I did that for about six months; I lost maybe forty pounds and felt incredible about it. This is it, I thought; I'm done forever.

But like any other diet, it ends; then I gained back even more than I had lost. It reignited the eating disorder. I became obsessed with my body. I felt incredibly unattractive, and I drank a lot. I wasn't able to put it together how that fit in with the time in my life—just really acting out unhealthy behaviors. But it was manageable. Because I could point to my success in school—I got straight A's throughout all this obsessing over not being good enough—it seemed that I could convince myself that things were OK, and, of course, the rest of the world couldn't tell by looking at me that I had anything wrong with me. Not that there was anything wrong, but that I had a lot going on.

The second year there I sort of did the same thing—lost weight, gained weight—but on a smaller scale, but always in a very obsessed way. Not a day would go by when I wouldn't think about the size of my body. And what am I going to eat next? Or, What did I just eat? When I got to New York, it intensified again. I wanted desperately to blend in, so I started running. It was a new version of the eating disorder, where I didn't change my eating habits—I still ate a lot of food, I drank a lot—but I started exercising compulsively. I'd skip work to go running. I would get to work late; whatever it took, I would have to run, or I would just be out of my mind. I lost a lot of weight, invested a lot of money in clothes, trying to be a New Yorker.

I guess it all really came down on me when I moved to Santa Cruz and started my Ph.D. Again, all the insecurities flooded back: Am I smart enough? Will I ever finish? These people are better than me. I gained an incredible amount of weight. I was twenty-six, and I'd been dealing with this obsession for more than ten years. Being in Santa Cruz, where there's a lot of healing, therapy, I sort of tuned into that and started seeing a therapist, basically because I wanted to lose weight. I thought, *If I go to therapy, I'll lose weight, and then all my problems will be gone.* Of course, that didn't happen; instead I ended up gaining more weight initially because my therapist asked questions about things that I wasn't that interested in talking about or thinking about: things about my family and what it was like as a young girl to have my father leave—the feelings that a lot of people have about not fitting into the world.

So I simultaneously started my Ph.D. in anthropology and started seeing a therapist. It was an intense combination since I was doing an academic study of my home community on the reservation, my home town, while at the same time I was addressing incredibly personal questions in therapy regarding my feelings of guilt about being white and privileged and having the luxury of leaving my family and friends on the reservation to attend graduate school.

The third year of my Ph.D. program, I moved back home to do my fieldwork for my dissertation. Mainly, the fieldwork consisted of talking with people and doing a lot of historical and political research. Living there again as an adult with more of a national perspective on things was very healing and represented the beginning of my understanding of how the reservation fit into the national and world systems. I also came to terms with how historical forces and questions of identity continue to shape the way Indian people are constituted as political subjects. So there I was: a white anthropologist getting a Ph.D. at a prestigious university—someone who, at least on the surface, was a participant in the power structure—yet I was also a member of the community I was studying. I wanted to use my unique position both to tell the truth and work out how I felt about wanting to "escape" the very community that I now embraced. I had to come to terms with both parts of my own history. I was both a legitimate resident and a privileged white person, so now what was I going to do about it? I finally got to the point of asking, "So what?" and wanting to make something useful out of that paradox.

So I quit worrying and started writing and speaking about how my presence on the reservation exposed a hidden history of non-Indians living on reservations, using resources supposedly reserved for Indians, that Indian reservations are not economically or politically isolated and therefore poverty cannot be blamed on tradition, but must be explained through a world systems approach. In other words, I decided to take the dissertation in a new direction. Rather than stay on the quite useless question of "Why do I feel this way?" I realized I could move to a political and historical position that had some meaning beyond my own tiny life. It was an incredible insight and a metaphor, I think, for the work I am doing now.

Just before I turned thirty, my life took on a whole new urgency. I decided to clear things out; whatever wasn't working had to go. I started seeing someone who really opened me up sexually. That was a really significant move for me. It actually opened up a whole other world. It gave me the permission. I was exploring my body, getting massage, and experiencing pleasure—not just sexual pleasure but that my body could be a vehicle for pleasure. That was something I had never considered. I had always considered my body as a barrier between me and other people. It was as if I was in there somewhere and people would try to get to me and couldn't. It was so isolating.

Through those years of therapy, I started to experience myself completely differently, where my body became the vehicle for pleasure or for expression. Instead of something blocking other people and me from meeting, it was the way that we could meet. I had never considered that and certainly never experienced it. I got really excited about it. At the time, all these things were happening, I was also having incredible grief, which is a very physical process: chest pains. The emotional burden is such a physical one as well that I feel that even eating was overburdening my body. Like my body was so burdened with emotional digestion that adding food to it was too much. It was an incredible time when I needed to be nurtured, and I found someone who was able to help me do that. It was incredibly healing. I feel that I've reached a point of real clarity. Now it's time for me to put that clarity to action. It's one thing to know things, understand them, but now I have to really live that way. And I'm doing that so far.

That year I turned thirty was a year of incredible changes. My brother died in February; I ended a long-term relationship in March; I started seeing a man and changed my whole sexuality in terms of how I was living in the world; I finished writing my dissertation, packed up my stuff, and drove across the country to Washington, D.C., where I was going to make my political move and change the world—or at least engage with it.

So I got to Washington, and four weeks to the day, I had a job interview with a national commission studying exactly the thing that I had just finished writing my dissertation about two months earlier, which was casinos on Indian reservations. I had done an analysis of this commission in my dissertation because it's such a huge development in the history of Indian affairs. So I had done a policy analysis, following the crafting of the legislation that set up this commission; I had been following it for two years. And certainly I had never considered that I would be working for them. If anything, I figured I would be moving to Washington, maybe writing *about* them, certainly not writing *for* them. I just felt that was another in a long line of validations.

I had studied something that didn't seem to have any practical value at all, but was interesting from an anthropological perspective. I'm now writing basically on the same topic, but instead of going to my dissertation committee, this document is going to Congress and to the president and is going to have a real impact on policy.

I feel incredibly fortunate and enthusiastic about it. The job has allowed me to meet and spend significant amounts of time with the top people in Washington in Indian affairs—people I've read about and written about, and now they know me by name. And I know them. It's been an incredible beginning for the thirties decade. I get overwhelmed at the possibilities. It seems I have come full circle, and I have been able to integrate my personal, professional, and academic lives in a way that allows me to really affect things.

Maybe the big theme of the thirties for me is going to be coming to terms with some sort of creative way to have a partner. What I'm looking for is a companion, an equal, a co-conspirator in the world, someone who will walk next to me, who won't be in my shadow behind me but also won't be in front of me in my way. I feel those are the only two positions that have been filled for me so far: someone's either in my way, sort of tripping me up, holding me up, or standing behind me, complaining about being in my shadow and wanting me to shrink to his or her size. I really want someone who will be next to me, equally embracing for the world. I have an ideal. In my weaker moments, I do get scared that I'll settle, but I have a lot of great friends, very strong, honest friends, who, I trust, will at least point out what's happening, if not try to get involved in stopping it. (I understand no one can stop me.)

I've been looking for simple answers rather than looking for answers, looking for meaning. Those are two really different goals. All these other attempts were to answer things and to realize now that there may not be answers; it's more honest to look for meaning. I'm not going to solve the body question, but I can inquire into what it means, how it functions to mask other concerns or fears. What does it all mean that I'm doing this? I think that's a really useful distinction to make between answers and meaning. That is maybe a very succinct way to describe what I've been trying to articulate. I spent my twenties looking for answers and only in the year when I turned thirty, when all this upheaval came, did I realize there weren't any and that I was asking the wrong question. Instead of saying, "What is the answer?" I should have said, "Why or how can this be meaningful?" and not looking for solutions anymore.

There's a clarity because I'm not looking for simple answers. That really resonates with what I feel my thirties are going to be about. I'm looking for meaning in my career. I don't just want to make money. I'm looking for meaning in a relationship, not for the relationship to answer things for me. Rather, I want the relationship to bring meaning into my life in terms of connection and soul searching, make me a better version of myself—those kinds of things, not, *How am I going to pay my bills or get a house, and I need another person to do it.*

Another way that I was searching, was moving around a lot. I moved from Mahnomen to Minneapolis, to Honolulu, to Minneapolis, to Honolulu, to Washington, D.C., to New York City, to Santa Cruz, to Mahnomen, to Santa Cruz, to Washington, D.C., in twelve years. That's a lot of moving. I plan to stay in Washington, D.C. I'm willing to consider moving, but I don't plan to move. That represents another reincarnation of looking for meaning. But the emphasis on the looking—where do you look? Do you look in places, or do you look inside? Do you look in your environment or your people? Somehow I felt that I had to go and find out; now I want to stay put and find it, create it. That's another distinction that I foresee for myself. I no longer have to rush around the globe wondering what I have missed. I am finally a full participant, so I can stay put.

*If there's anything I've had to grapple with in my thirties, it's the notion of achievement being so all-important and what that really means. I'm sure it's different things to different people, but I think I'm finally seeing what it really means to me. It's more intangible. It's not how much money I have in the bank, or what kind of car I drive, or where I go for vacation. It's more like, Do I have enough time for me and mine? Am I striking a good balance?*

MIMA LECOCQ

# Mima Lecocq

## PROFILE

This was no "Frankie and Johnny" diner dive; it was class. It was Chez Panisse. Mima Lecocq had been waitressing her way through the University of California at Berkeley in comparative literature and her second language, French. Although she was living with her boyfriend, one Monday morning when Tom McNary, the new cook, walked in, she began "lusting after him." They worked together during the day, with him filling her orders, and they catered together at night.

Six months later, Tom moved on to a new restaurant, and Mima, after graduating from Berkeley, moved to the other side of the counter, as a cook. A year later, Tom moved in with Mima. A year after that, they decided to try their skill at their own food business near Santa Cruz, California. They opened a charming American charcuterie, Carried Away, specializing in take-out.

Seven years after they'd met at Chez Panisse, they were married. Mima jokes, "People ask, 'What could be so romantic about being in business together that would make you want to get married?' That's not the idea. It's not that it's so romantic; it's that we finally got around to it. We finally had a little time and a little money and the energy to do it."

Now, four years later, Mima sits before me, nine months pregnant and having irregular contractions, talking with me about her marriage, her son, her business, and the impending birth of her daughter, Olivia.

## The Gift of Motherhood

If there's time and energy and money for more children later on down the line, I'd just as soon adopt them. Actually I wanted to adopt this one, but it was kind of prohibitive money-wise. Tom has a cousin who runs an adoption agency in San Francisco that specializes in placing children of color, and I looked into it. Aside from costing ten thousand dollars or more, there are also a couple of scary factors, like a mom's being able to change her mind and that kind of thing. So Tom didn't want to do it for those reasons. Actually, it's cheaper and easier to have your own. If someday we can have more, that's the way to do it. Both Tom and I are adopted, so it would have been a really fantastic legacy to continue.

I grew up in Kensington, California, on Ocean View. My mom and dad adopted me when I was a couple of months old, but then the adoption agency kept me for two extra months under supervision because my head was too big. This has been a great source of family jokes! I guess I came home when I was about four and a half months old, which is a trip to me, since now I know all that happens in those first few months of life. My mom was telling me the other day that I slept through the night and never cried. I don't think that that necessarily bodes well for what may have happened before I came home. I think Tom too came home at six months. He went to a couple of foster homes; he was slightly antisocial. I thought he was mean when I first met him. But he's really supersoft and sensitive.

My sister's adopted too, and is three years younger than me. My mother had tuberculosis when she was eighteen, so she couldn't have children. I don't know what that has to do with the reproductive process, but that's how she's always explained it. Mom and Dad split up when I was in sixth grade. I was kind of relieved because there was a lot of fighting at my house. But it was sad. I was sort of precocious as a kid. I kind of absorbed things as a mini-adult, and consequently a lot was expected of me. My mother would put me in the middle of things. We learned to do all those kinds of things when we were real little. When she opened the bakery, we were in charge of running the house. We would alternate cooking dinner every night.

I got into loads and loads of trouble. Boys and drugs. I didn't go to class (it was hardly challenging). Finally I got into a little bit too much trouble, so they shifted me off to France for a year. It saved me. I got into more trouble there, but at least it was sort of enlightening while I was at it. I knew some French, but I learned it a lot better. I was at a boarding school for wayward kids—an international school, really cool. There were kids from Africa and all sorts of French-speaking countries. It was fun. It definitely broadened the proverbial horizons. I almost got kicked out from there a couple of times. I'd skip classes, sneak out all night. I ran away a couple of times—hitchhiked to Paris, got busted by the cops. Anything I could think of. I didn't care about anything.

I did a lot of acid in my early teens; then when I was getting into trouble with boys, it was more like speed and stuff. Thank God, all that stuff's over with. In my twenties I did a ton of coke too, so I must have a pretty addictive personality. You run the gamut, get it out of your system. Now it's just food; now it's just work. When I came back, I shaped up my act, went to college prep.

I started busing tables at Chez Panisse when I got out of high school and went to UC Berkeley, then worked at Café Fanny for a little bit, went to France again for a little bit, and then came back and waitressed, so I was mostly in the front of the house. But then when I was almost finished in school and I had met Tom and we were thinking about getting into the food business, I thought, *Well, I should work at cooking a little bit professionally to see if that's really what I want to do.* When I was finishing up school, I started working in the kitchen at Chez Panisse, maximum two years. Money's a lot better waitressing! But I was having fun doing it and being with Tom on that side of the line. We knew that was what we wanted to do. That was cool. Then I got some money from my dad. He said, "It's either for graduate school or for a business." Pretty fortunate, huh? I tease him now that I should have used it for graduate school.

My mom, Lilly Lecocq, moved down here about six months after we did. We were talking to Mark and Kelly, who own Kelly's bakery, about our plan, and they asked why we didn't consider doing it down here, so we came down and checked it out. We thought it would be good because the area's not as saturated with food businesses, so it's less competitive—which has turned out to be kind of true, but it also has its drawbacks. I don't think the consciousness is what it is in the Bay Area, so there's not as much exposure and so forth. By the same token, you can just do your job and not need as much innovation or PR.

The business evolved pretty organically. It's been ten years. It hasn't made us rich or famous, but it provides us with a decent living and a great lifestyle.

Now that we don't work all the time, it's hard to think about doing anything on a grander scale. We have this serious family to provide for now. We're getting a little older; we ought to think about making some more money. We oughta, oughta oughta. But we're kind of relaxed. There are times when we work like dogs, of course, but for the most part, we're in the groove. Tom went two years in a row to the Bohemian Grove on the Russian River to cook, so he leaves me to run the fort for two weeks in May and three in July. He makes a lot of money there. I booked a ton of weddings last year before I knew when he would be gone. This year I did know in time and knew I was pregnant, so I booked only a couple, but regardless, it's totally grueling. That's when we work like dogs.

The business is quasi-successful. Depends on how you qualify or quantify it. We have a good crew; we have a good job; we're in demand. There are times where we have cash crunches. It's not doing so well that I don't worry about the bills being paid off, but it can be more or less run without my being there on a daily basis too. That's worth a lot. We are off Sundays and Mondays. He works on Saturdays, and I work on Tuesdays. We get two and a half days off each and two altogether as a family. Pretty luxurious. We live five minutes from here too, so we don't spend a bunch of time on the road.

The other thing that I'm ready to do is a cookbook when I can find the time. I have good connections to get it launched. There are two things I know well enough and have enough recipes for and have developed over the last ten years that I think are original enough: a salad book and a dessert book. I have to see about the salability, but I have a friend who coached me who knows a lot. Those projects need time.

I also do some magazine writing. I'm pretty proud of that. It's kind of a hard thing to crack. It's been fun and definitely satisfying egowise, but I need to pursue it a little more. After I have the baby, I'll work on a couple of more proposals. I have a good feeling for what they want, but they also have plenty of really good writers. You have to be patient to get your stuff in and plenty humble. Compared with the Paul Bertollis [the well-known Berkeley chef] of the world, I'm nobody, so I've gotta find something that works for them and that works for their timeliness. Magazine writing isn't going to be a career. Tom always thinks I ought to try to make it one, but I don't have the perseverance.

I could also do a cookbook for children. That's more unusual with more of a market. But I'd want to get more experience under my belt. It'd be a dream. Then we would want to build a kitchen, when we buy our own house, just the way that I want it for the kids. But I may as well start off doing it any old where and see if I really do like it first. You're doing certain things for awhile and you're pretty full in life, and the projects are hard to implement, so I'm just doing the thinking part of it now. I'll start putting the specifics on paper after the baby comes and see what my energy limitations are.

Being a mother the last four years has been illuminating. It's taught me a lot about what's important and about myself. That sounds very vague, I know. In a nutshell, I used to be driven by a lot of stuff on the exterior, and it's sort of shifting inward. Now, having a child teaches me to be more driven by what's inside. The external is like getting things published and putting money in the bank, putting on the proper dinner party. Now it's about being able to focus my attention, shutting off from work and going to the beach. That "present" thing. The "to-do list" needs to get chucked in the garbage occasionally and totally ignored. What's important is how you spend your energy and what you teach your kids. Not teaching—kind of guiding. Marlon has such a sweet disposition naturally, but I think he was just meant to be compassionate and empathetic. I don't really need to show him much, but I like seeing that he's somehow learning right. He's so good in swim lessons that they call him Fish Boy. I like watching him get all excited about the fact that he's going to have a little sister. I know we're going to have our moments; I'm not like totally naive. He talks to my belly—talks about how he's going to let me help him with Olivia. He's already such a big boy and so independent. How is he going to be? Such loads of fun.

I have no complaints about my marriage. None. I'm happier in it than I could have ever dreamed. I dropped Marlon off at his preschool this morning. There was a kid crying, and he's probably older than Marlon. I hadn't noticed the kid having a hard time before, so I asked one of the teachers: "Is it because he has a new baby sister?" She said, "Yeah, there's a lot of stuff. His dad's not around anymore." I'm like, "Oh, but there's a new baby." She said, "Different dad." I was thinking that is so rough, so rough.

We are such a little unit at our house; we're all so tight. Lo and behold, I'm listening to the radio boppin' down here, and I hear Al Green's "Let's Stay Together." I'm almost in tears, thinking I'm so damn lucky. We've been married seven, eight years, been together about twelve. We've been together a third of my life, I figured out the other day. Who would have thought? I sure wouldn't have. I never stayed with anybody for terribly long before Tom and didn't think I could be content in that kind of situation.

That's another reason it took us a long time to get married: I didn't think I could be married, and here I am—happily, happily married. He asked me fairly early on, and I said, "I don't think so," and then he didn't ask again for a long time. Actually I think I said, "Do you still want to? Because I think I'm ready now if you want to." Then he was reticent, of course. I don't blame him either, watching people get married and break up.

I think about problems or hurdles I've had that I feel I've done a pretty good job with, and it's still a battle. We all have those internal tapes playing, those little demons we have to fight. If there's anything I've had to grapple with in my thirties, it's the notion of achievement being so all-important and what that really means. I'm sure it's different things to different people, but I think I'm finally seeing what it really means to me. It's more intangible. It's not how much money I have in the bank, or what kind of car I drive, or where I go for vacation. It's more like, Do I have enough time for me and mine? Am I striking a good balance? Am I not waking up at night worrying about stupid stuff? If I had problems that maybe other women in their thirties might be having or have had, it's just about how to get over those kind of fears. Fear of failure or fear that you might not be as successful as you thought you wanted to be at one time.

That initial drive for me came from my mother, which is good. I got that good strong work ethic from her. I got the desire to be a perfectionist. All of that is good, and sometimes lacking with people to a degree, but to where it rules you and makes you afraid, it's not a good thing. She had superstrict, strong expectations of me. The tape that I've worked to shut off in my head is the "It's not good enough" tape. I am just about over that; that tape is almost done.

What helped me to disconnect the tape was just getting to be such a wreck from it that nothing made sense anymore. It was absolutely useless. I was no good as a wife or a mother or a friend or anything, because I was just too caught up in being good enough. It's not like it happened overnight or anything, and it's had its painful moments, but just letting go of that garbage. It's funny because everything's still the same except for the anxiety that accompanies all that. Everything still gets done. Everything still works out.

The struggle's not over, and sometimes when I get real caught up and I have a lot of work to do, it's harder to back off from it and not get caught up in it again. I always started everything kind of early in my life and packed it all in. I'm probably still a little bit ahead of the time frame. Or maybe it just got so intense there for awhile that it had to run its course a little bit faster. For some people, the thing is more gradual. I spent a year where I got myself into a totally wrecked shape worrying about everything. I just dealt with it. I went to therapy for about three or four months before Marlon was born, so I had some sense of what the root causes of it were. I remembered during that year of being caught up in all that anxiety, so I used what I learned in therapy: common sense, introspection, the help of having a super partner to talk everything through with. For being such a grump, he actually has a remarkable sense of acuity when it comes to that kind of thing. I don't know if that's advice, but a lot of girlfriends around my age are all struggling to "achieve," and we all have our moments like this. I don't know if everybody's has to get as bad as mine was, but if that is kind of a common phenomenon, I think it's something people need to work at to minimize, if not eliminate.

My mom's a fantastic grandma. She and our son have a really, really special relationship. She watches him two days a week. After we had Marlon, things got a lot easier because her focus wasn't on us anymore; it was on him. Only recently, actually, have we touched on those sensitive spots between us. I love her dearly, but I've come to the realization that there are certain things that she will never understand and that I'm better off not even trying to work through them with her.

Recently we had a fight because I thought that if everything went well for the birth of this baby, I would have my friend bring Marlon to watch his sister being born—just the last part, not the whole grueling labor. It was just a maybe, but she disagreed vehemently on this idea for a bunch of reasons. She was just being protective of him. I understand that. But she did not respect at all any of my ideas on the matter. I don't even know if she heard them in the first place. I thought, *Oh God, that's just her—her old stubborn European controlling ways.* But then she hurt me because I said, "OK, Mom, I know what you're saying, but you know whose decision it will be ultimately." Oh, she hated that. I said it in a gentle way, but then she went for below-the-belt comments about me: "You always just think about how things are going to enhance you only." I just went, "Whoa, what are you saying here? You mean I'm not thinking about the welfare of my son first and foremost? You're nuts. That's below the belt." I tried to ignore it for awhile.

Finally we had a fight like we haven't had since I was a teenager. I said, "You just can't say things like that to people. You can't do that to people you love—talk to them that way." She wouldn't admit to having done anything wrong to save her life. I just have to let her be that way. It's not that there was a fight and someone has to win either. I was only trying to make her understand how badly she hurt me. If someone told you that you were thinking about yourself before your kid, it would hurt. So I'm like, "OK, fine, fine, fine. I wasn't just not going to let you know how much that hurt me; that's all I can do."

I don't really consider my mother a role model as much on an emotional level. She grows things in her garden and makes herself a little dinner every night and takes a hot tub and goes to the market on Saturdays—that's sweet and nice, but it's pretty solitary. I would rather not be by myself, and the other thing is that I don't know that I wouldn't want something a little bit more fulfilling spiritually or emotionally. She's closed off to so many ideas. It's a hard thing to put into words. She can be kinda myopic. I don't want to have my system be as closed as that when I get to be that age. I still want to question things and explore things. She's too set in her ways. I know that's definitely a generational thing too. I notice that the people my age and even younger are exploring more about themselves and their place in the world than ever before. I think I was taught to be real stoic and unquestioning and follow certain principles and guidelines. I'm kinda rejecting that. She still lives and breathes those rules, so that's a main way in which I would not want to follow in her footsteps. Maybe I'm on just a little bit of a negative jag with her right now, but overall, she does have a lot and has taught me a lot about how to enjoy the stuff that's out there: doing things, having fun, those kind of experiences.

I had never thought about aging, but the other day I did because I think of Tom's mom, who is dying of cancer. I was thinking about how many years she had versus how many I have. Plus she said to me on the phone, "You have the most important part of your life yet to come," meaning raising my children. While I know that to be true, it's like, wow, that certainly is very, very precious. I don't want, on my deathbed, having regrets about how I spent my time, so it kind of forced me to think about it. Not that I've come to any conclusions whatsoever, except just to cherish it. I'm pretty content with the fundamentals of what I have. I don't need to find the right husband or finish my education or anything like that. Aging is something I'm just starting to broach. We have plans of things we want to do, but they're sort of frivolous—places we want to go, things we want to do with the kids, and all of that. But that's not really aging.

I don't have a problem with my pregnant body at all. Thankfully, I have a husband who doesn't either; he loves it. It hasn't been tedious or too cumbersome or had health problems associated with it. But I do have a little bit of a problem otherwise—not having my cute nubile teenage body that I used to have. After Marlon, I never got back down to what I used to be in my prime. It's not a huge issue, but I'm vowing to myself that after this pregnancy I'm gonna get a personal trainer if I have to. I probably won't. It's just finding the time and discipline. I know I'm not twenty anymore; that's just the way it is. It would be nice to wear that cute, skinny-tight clothing that I have in my closet. I haven't parted with it yet; still hoping.

Olivia will be able to wear it in a few years. I'll be jealous. I can see where I'm gonna have problems in about fourteen years. I'll have to live vicariously through her. I don't have any huge issues with it, but I sure would like to be fit and cute again some day.

A lot of my girlfriends are in angst: "Should I have children; should I not? Can I have children; can't I? Will I meet the man; won't I?" It was always a given for me that I would have children. Even before I knew I would be married, I knew I would have children. It hasn't been anything unusual; I did it with some thought but mostly instinct. Being a parent doesn't cause me much consternation. That's easy for me.

A friend who was just visiting has been HIV positive for fourteen years, but there is a 1.5 percent chance that the virus will be transmitted to the baby. She's resolving her fears and going to try. Nothing needs to be said to her. She's in such good health.

Another friend was scared and worried about her abilities as a mom. What do you say to somebody like that? You have to work that out for yourself. Now she has a baby, and I think it's just all falling into place naturally. Sometimes people think about things too much. Whether or not to have children—it's a huge responsibility. It's better than not thinking at all and just doing it.

But I will say that I don't understand the women in their late thirties or early forties who have never had children and they've really had only themselves or maybe a relationship, but then it comes to a point where they feel they don't want to give up their freedom. They see it as giving up. I don't understand it. I couldn't relate to it, and I couldn't even begin to respond to it. It's so antithetical to my way of being. I hear that too. In my prenatal yoga class, we have check-in time before we start doing yoga. I hear a lot about women's concerns—they're already pregnant, but they have fears and misgivings. That's something I just can't relate to because I wasn't worried about it for myself and because it comes so naturally to integrate a child into my life. They are afraid to give, when being a mother gives to *you,* the mother. The amount of effort expended is nothing compared to what you get out of it.

*Surround yourself with people who say "yes" or "why not?" to your deepest dreams and help you figure out how to achieve them. You are not wrong in wanting to pursue a dream that is personal to you. If you're feeling it, visualize it, draw it, paint it, write it, say it, dance it. Trust yourself, and get some support.*

RANDI GRAY KRISTENSEN

# Randi Gray Kristensen

## PROFILE

When I first asked Randi Gray Christensen about her lifestyle in the multicultural Adams-Morgan neighborhood in Washington, D.C., she replied, "If I were to sum up my lifestyle, 'simple' would probably do it. I aim for Bob Marley's invitation to 'live the life you love, and love the life you live.'" Although she confesses to not "always hitting the mark." Randi describes herself as an introverted bookworm who likes to play and socialize without too much planning. She lives with her cat, Shadow, in a studio apartment loaded with bookshelves in a multiethnic, mixed-class neighborhood that is jammed with cafés, restaurants, clubs, and bookstores. "So," she smiles, "I can curl up here as long as I like, and when the urge hits me, city life is at the doorstep."

I met Randi when she taught her first course at Pacifica Graduate Institute, where I am completing a Ph.D. in mythological studies. The class, Cultural Mythologies I: Textual Healing in New World African Literatures, was described as an exploration of the link between individual and communal healing as it is examined through the prism of literary representations of the experiences of peoples of African descent in the New World. I liked her immediately. I liked her noncommittal, Mona Lisa smile, which never quite lets you know what she's thinking. But also I was drawn to her natural warmth and easy laugh, which often soften her direct, hold-no-prisoners stance.

Randi's passion was observing the rearticulation in literature of mythologies, rituals, and practices that circulate and recirculate throughout the Americas and West Africa and develop within, against, and in creative recombinations with those of various European and Native American peoples. The class was a concentration on the specific qualities and expressions of the New World African mythologies and was an introductory exposure to novels, poems, plays, and critical analyses that deliberately address the relationships of myth, history, and ritual to personal and, by extension, community transformation among peoples of African descent in the New World. Her reading list ranged from Ntozake Shange's *For Colored Girls Who Have Considered Suicide When the Rainbow Is Enuf* and August Wilson's *Joe Turner's Come and Gone* to Toni Cade Bambara's *The Salt Eaters*, and Paule Marshall's *Praisesong for the Widow.*

Randi, who has an M.F.A. in fiction, also teaches at St. Lawrence University and, for her Ph.D. in African American and Caribbean literatures, is completing a dissertation on marronage in novels by black women writers, as both a historical and psychic process. She says happily that her creative juices are coming back now as the dissertation winds up.

An ethnic mixture of Danish-Jamaican-American descent, Randi was raised in both Washington, D.C., and Jamaica. She feels that her life has been occupied by two questions: Why are things the way they are, and How do you change them? She is doing her part to reconcile the link between individual and communal healing.

# A Solitary Journeyer in Community

Basically, I'm a Danish-Jamaican-American, raised by my Jamaican mother and grandmother in both Washington, D.C., and Jamaica. By the time I graduated from high school, I had attended six schools in eleven years and knew how to negotiate customs in three languages and on two continents. So my upbringing was characterized by geographical and cultural change, often bewildering, and not of my choice. My subsequent life has been characterized by geographical and cultural change, often bewildering, but fueled by my choice!

I think early on I was caught by two questions: Why are things the way they are, and How do you change them? More specifically, from my child's perspective, why are people so mean to outsiders, and what makes the nice ones different from the mean ones? I'd say my work has been about refining those questions and their possible answers, and it just happens to be occurring at a time when those questions, in their more refined state and brutal expression, are very alive.

Having always been an outsider and experiencing superficial and deep relationships with folks who experience themselves inside some kind of identity, as well as with other "outsiders," I thought at first that education was the key. It seemed to me that many of the things people clung to in order to define themselves were pretty arbitrary—who we worshipped, how we looked, how we ate, what language we spoke—and certainly not something to hate others over. But I also seemed to know that it wasn't about lecturers in a hall telling people to be nice to other people because they should. I turned to cultural work because it seemed to reach past words to something felt, whether through the sound of a voice chanting poetry, or music that tickled the rib cage, or art that made you cry or laugh, those aha's of recognition that didn't erase differences, but made connections with something in someone else, and someplace inside too, and in turn shifting the perceptions of the differences, didn't make them less real, but less life threatening, less dangerous, less needing to be eradicated, perhaps even valuable, and adaptable, and if not translatable, at least respected. Those are small, intimate moments, but extremely difficult to create and rescue from powerful historical and economic forces that have depended on, and continue to depend on, mutual hatred and fear in order to maintain control, and more than willing to sacrifice people in horrific ways in order not to lose control, or be changed.

My work seems to be about finding ways to name those forces—white supremacy, racism, poverty, misogyny, homophobia, capitalism, Eurocentrism, religious fundamentalism—and their alternatives—communitas, marronage, interdependency, love, humility, reciprocity, exchange, recognition—in a lot of different settings, all pretty marginal: universities, community centers, independent bookstores, national nonprofit organizations, women's organizations, theater groups, poetry readings, and so on. I've spent much of my life so far learning from other people's ways of articulating those forces; more and more of that work is taking the form of my own writing—both are critical. Those voices have fed mine, like underground springs, and now mine is entering the flow.

It also seems to be finding a focus in classroom teaching, at the graduate and undergraduate levels, offering the views made available through the lenses tendered by African and African diasporic creative artists, to me powerful because they enable the intimate critiques and visions of possibility of the outsider—within Western culture. It makes them more difficult to dismiss. They hold both inside and outside simultaneously and offer choices. Toni Morrison said it best for me: "We are not others. We are choices."

As a nine year old, I went to boarding school in the mountains of Jamaica. I think that was my first complete experience of the topsy-turviness of many things. I had some glamor because I was coming from the States, but I was also aware that I was working class in the States, while many of the other students were truly rich. That class mattered between people was made clear, but it was an easy enough line to erase as a child. Color was a different issue; my grandmother was dark skinned, and it was confusing to my classmates that my grandma looked like their maid, and it was confusing, I think, to my grandma and other dark-skinned folks, both students and relatives, that I looked like those other folks. Add to that that it was an all-girls boarding school with tons of preadolescent and adolescent hormones running around, and very little, like NO, real information, and sexuality became polymorphous too—although it was made clear that we were to grow up to be ladies.

But for all of that, it was a time of enormous freedom. We were without direct adult supervision most of the time, and we had enormous territory to play in, and for me, as an only child, having automatic playmates twenty-four hours a day and seven days a week was fantastic. We wrote and performed plays for each other, competed hard academically and athletically, were by turns mean, scary, and totally absorbed in each other. I lived those two years flat-out and full speed at school. A friend who was raised on a kibbutz said that when Bruno Bettelheim studied kibbutz children, who were also raised away from their immediate family, they wound up with enormous peer loyalty. I have that across all kinds of borders—an independent core that's still with me—and a lived experience of freedom to invent that has also stayed with me. It made me a disrespecter of norms that has produced unending conflict in my life—some of it productive, some of it not. It also taught me the subversive power of laughter. And how to live through punishment.

There has been a more recent and profound transformation that has been slow but has had its moments. I was raised by strong black women whose deepest claim in this life is to have endured. My grandmother was born poor in Jamaica in 1900, my mother in 1922. There hasn't been a century since the beginning of the Middle Passage that hasn't been a holy terror for black people, and this one has been no exception. But my grandmother crossed over to the other side in her own home in 1988, and my mother still travels the world and has her own home, so the value of endurance has been bred in my bones. It has carried me far; I surely rely on it, and I give thanks for it. At the same time, the conditions of my life have a few more options than my grandmother's or my mother's. Thanks to their visions and commitments, I'm well educated (some would say overly educated), know how to make a living, am able to live closer to an alignment of inner desires and outward expression than they had the luxury of. So it was a shock to me to wake up at age thirty-six in a job where I felt totally depleted, in a community with no concern for my well-being. The words, "This is just too hard," were not part of my family vocabulary, but I felt flooded with relief by acknowledging them. I felt I was recognizing a space that wasn't even an option for them and generations before them, although they knew it must exist, and endured the invisibility and depletion I was feeling, waiting for it to be reclaimed. Within the aspect of the Caribbean women's tradition I had been raised in, I had gone "soft"—not a good thing. And this came in a cultural moment when we're not supposed to blame or complain, when we're supposed to numb our anguish or uncomfortable insights, or see them as strictly reflections of nuclear family dysfunction. But I claimed that feeling, and then sought, slowly, to change my situation on a large scale. I was inspired by [Caribbean scholar and activist] Rhoda Reddock's saying, which she learned in South Africa: Given the choice between there is no way, and there must be another way, we choose to find another way.

I'm deeply moved now by the statues of Elizabeth Catlett, where she depicts black women sitting, or lying down, or just being still and thinking, and the quilts of Faith Ringgold, and I've always appreciated Fannie Lou Hamer's declaration that "I'm sick and tired of being sick and tired." I just hadn't lived its emancipatory power yet.

Certainly, I've most admired my mother. I don't know; I suspect we all admire our mothers first, and then experience a sort of excruciating separation as we grow up and have to reinvent that relationship. She was a survivor, determined to keep body and soul together, and she raised her daughter against enormous odds. So she invested me with the notions of both possibility and empowerment.

More public figures I admire are Ella Baker, Fannie Lou Hamer, Mahatma Gandhi, Nelson Mandela—people who've put their considerable energies into battles for justice and grounded in a deep, all-encompassing sense of humanity. Those scribbling women—Colette, Anaïs Nin, Audre Lorde, Adrienne Rich, Michelle Cliff, Paule Marshall, Toni Morrison, Alice Walker, Toni Cade Bambara (I could go on for a very long time here)—were the ones who dared to speak the unspeakable, or the usually unspoken, because it needs to be said. It represents what's missing that we also need in order to come into balance. Those men—Rilke, Donne, Eliot, Bettelheim, Robert Jay Lifton, Franz Fanon, Malcolm X, Derrick Bell (again, this could go on for a while)—weren't afraid to expose wounds and consider their meanings—not with an eye to quick fixes but to a deeper understanding of what their meanings signify. Those are more public, distant folks I admire.

More directly, I'm blessed to know numbers of people who are acting on their personal visions. In our twenties, many of us seemed to be in training, learning, absorbing, integrating possibilities. In our thirties, we seem to be becoming more focused, more concentrated, translating that learning into something expressive that's unique to us. It's as if we're taking on the question of what do we do? We learned in our twenties that there are many things we can do, so what is it that we can uniquely and genuinely bring to the table? I'm sure I'm projecting here, but I notice more of that, or various stages along that process, in my surroundings. And so I admire those folks on the road less traveled for their courage to express those visions, to take responsibility for that: the co-owners of Sisterspace and Books [a bookstore], for example, Faye Williams and Cassandra Burton; Earthlyn Marselean Manuel, the creator of Black Angel cards [a type of oracle]; the painter Randell Henry, quietly making amazing paintings in Baton Rouge. I don't want anyone to feel left out, but my courageous friends know who they are!

Someone called me one cold February morning to say Nelson Mandela was being released from jail. I tuned in and saw something I had prayed and struggled for, but had no real confidence of seeing in my lifetime. My engagement with the South African situation really started with the Soweto uprising in 1976. The sight of children my own age fighting back woke me up to the ability to participate in the world, to make a difference. The more I learned about South Africa, the more horrified I became. I was stunned that the world hadn't intervened yet. So I participated in all kinds of marginal activities related to racial justice in South Africa and the United States. Trying to get my university to divest. Marching for the Dr. King holiday. Helping to publicize South African poet Dennis Brutus. Showing films on South Africa to audiences of five or six. They were tiny acts. But they kept the notion that something could and should be done until the groundswell took over, and everyone started getting arrested in front of the South African embassy and it started to be news and international pressure came to bear at last. And on a cold February morning, Nelson Mandela walked out of jail.

It's still a story in the process of creation, but the Soweto uprising initiated me to both the necessity of change and my participation in the world, and Mandela's release validated those efforts. It revealed that no matter how quixotic or foolish those gestures might seem, there's no point in judging them. If we're fortunate, we'll see results in our lifetime, but even if we don't, that we see the vision and act on it is important. And no act is too small. I feel that's the most important thing I can pass on right now to the generation coming up. I feel they're being indoctrinated that it's only the spectacular that counts—the immediate conversion experience, the sudden dawning of the light—and enormous changes will follow immediately. You know, "We Are the World" and that sort of thing. That's one way to go, but it's not the only one. If you put on an event and only five people show up, yes, look at how the publicity went and think about how to get ten people next time, but don't rip yourself off by acting as if those five didn't count. They count.

I can only say what's been valuable for me, but maybe it will be helpful to someone else. Get a friend. Then get another one. Surround yourself with people who say "yes" or "why not?" to your deepest dreams and help you figure out how to achieve them. Lose the romantic vision of doing it on your own and proving anything to anyone else. That might get you started, but might not carry you through. Be prepared for some loneliness, some doubt, some fear—but try to find out what they're telling you. Make them name themselves. A named doubt may be an issue worth addressing, but it rarely means your vision isn't worth pursuing.

Find some way of centering yourself daily: meditation, journaling, music—something to help you concentrate your energies once a day and give your spirit a chance to speak privately with yourself. Be good to yourself, and honest about what that means for you: could be diet, could be exercise, could be more private time than you're accustomed to. Be gentle with yourself and others as you make whatever changes you need to in your life to pursue your passion. Some of your friends will have been waiting for that passion to emerge; others will have become accustomed to who you have been and find the changes disturbing. Some will do both. Hang in there.

I think women are particularly oriented to not creating disturbances in the field, to assist others in expressing their visions and postponing our own, or getting vicarious satisfaction from others' successes. This has gone on for too long. I can't even imagine what the world would look like if all women said, "I have a point of view on that," but I wouldn't mind finding out. A young woman I know has a T-shirt that reads "Well-mannered women don't make history." You are not wrong in wanting to pursue a dream that is personal to you. If you're feeling it, visualize it, draw it, paint it, write it, say it, dance it. Trust yourself, and get some support.

Given my druthers, I'd rather have more time than more money, so I tend toward work that lets me organize my own time or offers blocks of time off, like university teaching or activist work that's demanding in spurts. Right now, I'm finishing my dissertation without a grant, so this is kind of an anomalous year. My daily routine looks something like wake at eight, journal, write, read, work on the dissertation, run errands, work from 3 P.M. to 7 P.M. at a black women's bookstore (Sisterspace and Books) right around the corner from me, watch *Jeopardy!* with friends in the building, then work out in the building gym with a pal, then either read some more, go out, watch TV, whatever, 'til I fade around midnight. I'm contracted to write a manual for nonprofits on using electronic mailing lists for organizing work, so I put in some time on that. If it's a nice day and I'm in reading mode, I'll take myself out to lunch in the neighborhood before going to the bookstore. I'm learning how to pray. I walk to work and back for exercise. I've discovered Friday night dancing at a club down the street. Some of the neighbors from the building go there, so it's easy-going and friendly. The building's like a village in a village, and I'm starting to get the hang of it. The neighborhood gets invaded on weekends, sort of like Bourbon Street in New Orleans, so I tend to avoid it then.

There's starting to be a place or time for romantic love in my life, but that might just be spring in the air! My pattern's been relatively lengthy short-term love relationships, but I've been too much in flux to settle down or haven't found someone to "flux" with! In other words, I've never been much of a dater. The last couple of years have been full of dreams of laying down old structures and fondly bidding them farewell. I'm not sure what's going to arrive in its place, but I'm more of a respecter of feelings now than I was in the past and am just paying attention to them and seeing where they lead. So far, I'll dance flirtatiously with anyone, but you have to be doing something like writing poetry about marronage to really get my attention! I'm open, but I'm not rushing anything.

Some of my friends and I are tired of the expectation that romance and sex go together, and sometimes we extend a dead romantic situation just for sex. Sometimes you just want dessert without sitting through the seven-course meal. I felt a real pang watching *Living Out Loud* with Holly Hunter, when she hired a masseur to come to her apartment. I certainly prefer romance and sex to go together, but for me as a heterosexual woman, the one-night stand with a strange man feels too dangerous. I can't afford the masseur, and sometimes I just want sex. Haven't solved that one yet!

Most of my close friends are in the thirty-five to forty-five range. I have a few friends in their twenties, but there's something about crossing that bridge into the thirties that seems to make a difference in what we recognize in each other. In my twenties, I had a few role models among older women. Now I have fewer role models as such, but more people in general whose choices I admire and try to learn from. I seem to get more from perceiving folks as ordinary people doing extraordinary things, and paying attention to how they do that, and then looking at my own ordinariness and the choices I make, rather than role models on automatic extraordinary. I'm inspired daily by the sisters I work with at Sisterspace and the folks who come in there, for example. Shoot, on reflection, I seem to be learning from everyone I come in contact with!

Aging. It's already happening! I don't bounce back as rapidly as I used to from all kinds of things, my knees are shot, and I can't seem to get my metabolism started. So I guess my first perception of aging is the physical changes, the evidence of life lived on my face and my body. I've been relatively healthy in my adult life, so I haven't had to give a lot of energy to that kind of self-care, but I'm starting to pay closer attention to diet, exercise, moisturizer—all that stuff. I'm not that interested in my gray hair yet and get it dyed, but that feels more playful and self-pampering than anything else. I love getting my hair washed and my head massaged.

In the back of my head, the grasshopper and the ant fable surfaces more frequently, and I've identified more closely with the grasshopper so far in life. I'm feeling the next decade will be about consolidation as well as further exploration, to give the ant a little more equal time. I've just started realizing I'll probably live into my sixties at least, and while I've joked about living on my more stable friends' front porches in my older age, I wouldn't mind having a porch of my own for them to visit too.

Aging, or growing older, has been a positive experience for me so far, so I'm not really worried about it, as I struggle to name and integrate a chaotic personal and cultural history. My thirties have been about joy and pain and movement, greater inner flexibility, and outward expression, so my fantasy would be Auntie Mame in the end: flamboyant and daring and fearless and wearing very loud colors and embarrassing the young(er)! I'm not expecting to have children, but I'm counting on my friends to share theirs.

That's my inner vision. However, I'm also responding to these questions after the Colorado school shooting, and I'm not at all sure that the material and political comforts of living on the edge of the middle class as I have will extend into my old age. I feel as if the American monster of racial animosity is spreading its talons and getting a firm hold among the economically disenfranchised and providing stories of their misery that make sense to them, like it's black peoples' fault, or women's fault, or the fault of miserably paid Filipino workers that they haven't become Donald Trump—anything not to confront the economic disaster this conversion from a manufacturing to a service economy has produced. So the generation born in the Reagan-Bush years and the passionless Clinton years have been raised in an atmosphere of reckless disregard for human life, of "compassion fatigue" and other such nonsense, and are limited in their access to stories of change that make sense, that are new, that invite and inspire. Even those of us who benefited from the various civil rights movements of the sixties and seventies have been urged to join in the conspiracy of silence: to agree that everything's fine now, to endorse the dismantling of those feeble programs that have let us into the room though not into the conversation. I'm concerned about younger activists who tell me that they're more pragmatic than my generation, less interested in consciousness. Maybe they're relieved of some aspects of consciousness raising because they were raised in atmospheres where some of what we had to name was commonplace, like "women go to work." But I feel that pragmatics in the absence of a wider vision is extremely vulnerable and certainly no competition for the seductive pull of the white man's heroic journey against insurmountable odds, with God on his side, that the right has cultivated.

So I'm making no assumptions about "civil" society over the next few decades. I don't know which of these terrorist acts will be the awakening, or what that awakening will produce. Oklahoma City was plenty for me. I come from a culture with an activist strand that insists that none of us is free 'til all of us are free, and have felt that interdependence and responsibility all my life. Acting on that has brought great joy, and I've seen amazing changes in my lifetime. It seems to me that to continue that kind of work into one's thirties and over a lifetime winds up demanding a different way of looking at the world and at change.

In my twenties, there was this feeling that if I changed what was out there, then what was inside could have room to breathe. I've come to see that both had to happen: what was inside had to breathe out loud in order both to change things and to be changed, and what was out there had to be changed to make some breathing room for more of us, for more choices, for more alternatives. And that "inside" and "out there" were deeply intertwined in everyone. Those were words of convenience, but not really separate, and at some point viewing them as separate can obscure more than it reveals, just as not talking about them as separate can. There are fine and important shades of distinction between stubborn commitment and rigidity. I learned a lot from Toni Cade Bambara, particularly in her novel *The Salt Eaters,* but also from her life, about living with and for change. Also from Paule Marshall's work. There's a memoir on the shelf at Sisterspace entitled *No, I Won't Shut Up,* and I expect that will be one of my mottoes. One of my *Jeopardy!* pals is blind, and he was describing a friend not too long ago and said, "He has limited vision, but he uses it well." I thought I would be pleased to have someone say that about me at the end of my life.

For me, feeling most alive has two aspects, both quite different. One is when I'm writing, really writing, either standing in the river and it just flows through me, or standing ten miles away, my hand cupped to my ear, trying to hear the whisper of the gurgle. Total focus, total concentration, total surrender, sitting at my desk. Lose track of time, day, munch on clementines and coffee. The other time I feel most alive is when I'm physically exhilarated: falling into the rhythm of the hike, being caught up in the energy of a dancing space, great sex. It's like the antithesis of the writing high—utterly wordless. I guess in both cases it's like my persona falling open and something more powerful flowing through.

My birthday's in August, and since I've spent most of my life in school in some fashion, it's always been a time of beginnings for me. On my thirtieth birthday, I had two parties—one with friends in Washington a couple of weeks early and a second with new friends in Baton Rouge, Louisiana, where I'd moved to begin graduate school. I had been out of school for eight years and was very conscious of going back into an environment I'd found dangerous in the past, but with a new attitude and set of expectations. I felt I was beginning a journey, and that a decade later (forty-one was in my mind) I'd be living with the decisions I'd made during that time. Old and new friends in D.C. gathered for a combination birthday party–send-off, and we had a great time grilling on the balcony of my little apartment, reminiscing and telling jokes. In Baton Rouge, I made a Jamaican meal of curry chicken and rice and peas, and invited one friend, who would turn out to be an anchor during my time there, and another couple, and it was a combination birthday party–housewarming. I'd gotten a new haircut for my new life, and hated it! But I was full of anticipation, and excitement, which pretty well carried me through that first year.

My last birthday was a bust. I'd just moved back to D.C. and thought I'd have the energy to host a party, but changed my mind in about a day. Had dinner with an old friend, hoping to begin our reacquaintance, but she'd double-booked that night and had to go. I felt abandoned and uncared for and couldn't stop crying in the restaurant—great blobs of tears rolling down my face. I might have moved a lot, but it's still a stressor, so it wasn't all about my birthday and my friend. I quite enjoyed that in the end. I'd never made a scene in a restaurant before. Quite liberating. I often surprise myself. This morning I had an idea for a class for black women in a community setting using *The Artist's Way* and Black Angel Cards. Last night I expressed some anger at someone and found it made a difference. I'm so accustomed to relying on analytical correctness that I sometimes forget about the power of emotional honesty. My anger has often been so strong that it's had the tornado effect on those around me, to the point where I started swallowing it altogether. I'm learning to express it without having to erase the other person. This is a time of change for me, or rather coming out on the other side of letting go of some beliefs and structures, so I'm pretty regularly surprised these days!

Spirituality and religious practice have been a regular, if eclectic, part of my life. I don't mean to make it seem compartmentalized from other parts of my life, because I don't experience it that way. If anything, more and more of what I do seems to emanate from that space, but I've been a pretty solitary journeyer over the years and find myself looking for a spiritual community as one of those sites of nurturing. I'm encouraged by the resurgence of attention to spirit in the last twenty years and the new avenues emerging from reworking ancient or traditional forms of spiritual expression. I'm still a bit impatient for their expression in the world, but that's my stuff. In my dissertation, I am arguing that some black women writers of the Americas are describing a process of change and growth that is comparable to the maroon experience in the New World. Maroons were self-emancipated Africans or Afro-Creoles and their allies who left the plantation; entered geographical, spiritual, and communal wildernesses; and remade themselves and each other into free and resistant peoples. New arrivals often had to undergo ritual processes of transformation, in the form of lengthy apprenticeships or other ordeals, before being fully accepted into the existing community, which was in turn revitalized by their presence. *Maroon* was not merely a legal or external designation; it represented an internal transformation from chattel slave to free subject, a healing of the psychic wounds of enslavement, and a restoration of self-in-community. The history of marronage, as it's been named, is a subjugated history in New World cultures, often unknown or, if known, marginalized in order to be dismissed. In the last decade or so, though, the term *marronage* and its meanings, while contested, are starting to show up more and more. The kind of creolization, or adaptive creativity, it represents, both apart from and in relation to plantation creolization, is beginning to be explored, perhaps as a source of alternatives to the sense of entrapment that globalization, often a broader expansion of plantation norms, is producing.

Comparable to the history of marronage, the story of black women's survival, lo this half-a-millennium, has also been a subjugated history. I was drawn to trying to describe a relationship between the two because of explicit work in some black women's novels, most obviously Paule Marshall's *The Chosen Place, the Timeless People,* where the story of a maroon rebellion is the basis of a rural community's collective identity and which they offer as a gift annually in a carnival masque to the newly independent, neocolonized nation they inhabit. It also forms part of the internal discourse of Merle Kinbona, a central character in the novel, whose psychic fragmentation and paralysis reflect the struggle to negotiate and integrate the multiple histories in which her culture and her life are entwined. It is the lived experience of marronage, as described in the novel, that restores her agency in the world. That is, it changes from a story she tells to a story she lives in a contemporary context, in a recognizable rite of passage. This motif appears in other works by Marshall—*Praisesong for the Widow, Daughters*—but is most explicit in *The Chosen Place, the Timeless People,* and so that work is at the center of the project.

Marronage appears in more muted forms in other works, so I begin the study with Toni Morrison's *Beloved,* and rearticulate Sethe's breakdown and recovery through the lens of marronage and identify Sixo as the representative of marronage in her and Paul D's "re-memory" of him and of themselves. I close the dissertation with a consideration of Maryse Conde's first novel, *Heremakhonon,* where the central character goes to geographical Africa seeking the possibilities of marronage too literally and fails to recognize them or rather mistakes neocolonial African patriarchy for marronage, eventually perceiving her error and its sources.

There are, I think, a number of works that describe this process of personal and communal recovery—Sherley Anne Williams's *Dessa Rose,* Alice Walker's *Meridian,* Toni Cade Bambara's *The Salt Eaters*—explicitly from a black women's perspective. I'm not suggesting that this is the only reading available or that black men aren't writing something comparable. But I chose these three to focus on because I also wanted to offer a cross-cultural reading—from the United States to the formerly British-colonized Caribbean to the French-colonized Caribbean—to see if there was something in common within those differences, a counternarrative to the plantation discourse also arising within globalization. So that's all very scholarly, but the drive to take on such a project was also personal. I had heard stories of the maroons while growing up in Jamaica, although I didn't visit the maroon community of Moore Town until I was in my twenties. For me, whose existence is a contradiction to many of the empowered structuring categories through which many people make sense of the world, the stories represent hope, an opening, the possibility of recovering the humane from the inhuman, and re-visioning "contradiction" as "unresolved plurality," in the words of Caribbean poet Pamela Mordecai. To the point, they are stories I need. This history is also being drawn on by contemporary social movements, such as the Cimarron movement in Colombia, and the celebration of Zumbi and Dandara of Palmares, a maroon state in seventeenth-century Brazil that lasted longer than Yugoslavia, as part of Brazil's black consciousness movement.

Finally, it is also an opportunity for me to recover a spiritual experience that I almost missed or lost: the presence of the orishas, or divinities, who crossed over on the Middle Passage and have served, even as they are served, as the vessels of communal memory of an alternative ground for being.

Specifically, in this work I affiliate with Shango as the representative of distributive justice and Yemaya as the healing maternal as mythically informed metaphors for processes of marronage. But there are many others who are calling us to honor what we're often rewarded for forgetting. *Ashe!* [a Yoruba word for "power," as in "the vital force in all living and nonliving things"]

*To thine own self be true. You will pay a price, certainly, for every pursuit of every passion, but if you don't follow your passion to wherever it leads you, you will pay for it in different ways. The only regrets I have are the times I said no—when I should have said yes—out of fear.*

KATE NOONAN

# Kate Noonan

## PROFILE

Kate Noonan was born in Los Angeles, of a first-generation Irish American father and a mother of Native American heritage. These facts, she recognizes, have only recently entered into her life consciously. She has begun to see a similarity in the spirit of both cultures, rooted in a shared sense of psychic exile. She refers to her inheritance as "a legacy of yearning—for home, for a sense of belonging, for a landscape"—a landscape she most readily finds in language. The stories, songs, and photographs that Kate remembers best speak of "what is succumbed to, what is resisted, what is lost, and what remains of an identity surviving under oppression." And these are themes that reoccur in her writing. As a writer she concentrates on short fiction, but the larger body of her writing has been for the theater.

Kate's father was an actor, her mother a former dancer. She is the third child of four: two brothers and a sister. Her father died of a brain tumor in 1968, a month after her eighth birthday and three days after Martin Luther King Jr. was shot. At that point, Kate remembers, the family sort of disintegrated, "my mother becoming alcoholic, and we were left in the position of really having to find our own way, kind of raising ourselves." She began acting at the age of three, with the encouragement of her father, and that activity was always a place of order and safety for her, due, she thinks, in large part to the chaos of her home situation. In the theater, the expectations were always clear.

Remaining close to her love of theater, Kate teaches "Performance from Scratch" workshops two or three times a year for actors, writers, and directors who wish to create one-person shows or to develop ensemble works. She directs as well. For the past three years, however, her main work has been teaching inner-city kids with issues of trauma or violence in their lives. It is an arts-based program, called Dramatic Results, that incorporates poetry, drawing, photography, and some movement. "We are beginning to incorporate the Native American model of council as a method of communicating and teaching respect," said Kate. Their goal is to create a sacred space, encouraging curiosity and expression, and keeping the act of creating art viable and safe. She spoke of how moving it is to watch these children recognize and invent themselves through the images they create and the stories they tell, and how her life has led her to this profoundly satisfying work.

## A Well-Crafted and Deliberate Life

I have always, always been in love with language. I used to love to pray out loud and learned all the Catholic prayers before I started school. My grandmother thought I was fervently pious. But to me, God and the words were the same thing; they were inseparable. I loved to say the act of contrition because it sounded so dramatic and passionate. Robert Louis Stevenson's poem "Where Go the Boats?" are the first words I remember hearing; it kind of woke me up to the world, and it is the first poem I memorized, I loved it so much. The first story I remember that caught me was the "Snow Queen." There was a book with beautiful illustrations by Arthur Rackham. I remember one in particular of the girl throwing her red shoes into the river, a sacrifice in exchange for helping her find her lost friend. That image moved me to tears for years. When I was nine or ten, I found Samuel Beckett's *Texts for Nothing* in a trash can in Topanga Canyon. I still have the book; it has companioned me in the deepest sense since I first picked it up. It was like hearing a grandfather's voice and my own at the same time. I take it with me when I travel and read it like a prayer book, and know most of it by heart. Also film has always been important to me. From the time I was two or three, I watched everything I could, and I still do.

And, of course, music has also been important to me. When I was twelve, I used to hang out in a club called the Bla Bla Club, a wonderful haven for musicians. It booked only acts that played original music. They gave me a job working the door; I was a kind of twelve-year-old bouncer. It became my home and my family until I was eighteen and moved to New York.

I think I started out wanting to be Bette Davis or Katharine Hepburn, and somewhere along the line I decided I really wanted to be John Huston. When I was eighteen, I began studying acting with Stella Adler, who changed everything in my life. I had always loved to act, but it was all about personality in L.A.—personality and mimicking experience. I wanted craft. I knew instinctively that there was more to it. Stella introduced me to the world of ideas—content, theme—making acting a spiritual practice, taking a specific moment and, as she would say, "lifting it" to the universal, revealing the meaning, the truth. I learned character from her. She was a masterfully skilled observer of human nature. She was more than an acting teacher; she was really a life teacher. She said, "If you tell a lie on the stage, it should offend your soul." So the craft really came down to finding the larger truth and revealing it. Everything I learned from her applies to writing as well. I realized at some point that I was more interested in ideas than in actual performing.

I was never really an ingenue. I was a character actor from birth, so I knew I would have to create my own work, carve out a niche for myself somewhere. Peter Brooks was an influence. I loved that he would take a great piece of work that obsessed him, like *The Mahabarata,* and work on it for ten years. That kind of dedication was inspirational. I always wanted to work with him. Antonin Artaud. Jerzy Grotowski. All the process junkies intrigued me.

Tentatively, I started writing and performing my own work, mostly raw autobiographical performance pieces, and eventually I found Rachel Rosenthal, who was and is a kindred spirit and who had a thirty-year head start in the direction I was heading at the time. So she saved me from having to reinvent the wheel. In Rachel, I'd found not only a mentor but a great collaborator, who would educate and encourage my own process. I learned a lot from her about abstract art, dance, the ritual aspects of performance, how to create visual tension, how to tell a story with light. It's been an invaluable partnership. Deena Metzger, my writing teacher, is another inestimable influence and guide. She demands rigor and honesty, is brilliant and insightful and deeply kind.

Tess Gallagher, the poet, took an early interest in my writing and was encouraging and helpful in a gentle way. Her interest gave me the confidence to start writing seriously, to take myself seriously. Up until then, I felt that "writing" and "poetry" were rooms I was not allowed to enter. I've been doubly fortunate to have deep friendships with these women, which is a grace note in my life.

The events of 1968, the year my father died, all seem to blur together: the assassinations of Bobby Kennedy and Martin Luther King, Vietnam, and my father's death. I didn't go to my father's funeral, so I watched TV and grieved with the nation. I was glued to the coverage of the mourners and the processions, searching for a way to behave. I was also mesmerized by the coverage of the war, and I identified very strongly with the Vietnamese children, but was actually envious because their pain was so visible and mine was so invisible and inarticulate. I kept a secret scrapbook of images from *Life* magazine, *Time,* and *Newsweek* of the fleeing women, napalmed children, whose expressions were bewildered and resigned, and I gave myself tests of endurance: How long could I walk in the heat without water? How long could I eat only oranges? It was very private and secret.

My entire childhood was littered with the corpses of heroes. Janis Joplin, Jimi Hendrix, and Jim Morrison's deaths all profoundly affected me. Then the big earthquake happened in L.A. around the same time. Nothing was certain: the world was unsteady; not even the ground beneath my feet was trustworthy. And, of course, finally, John Lennon in 1980. I was in New York, a few blocks away, living at the YMCA. It was a bone-numbing, completely lonely time. I never felt so utterly bereft. I guess if I had to articulate how it affected me, you could say a lesson I took from this was that to tell your truth was imperative, but it just might cost you your life.

I live a pretty quiet life. I love my neighborhood—Echo Park—its diversity and quirkiness. On one corner there's a Buddhist Thai temple, across the street is a Guatemalan Charismatic Baptist church, a Korean bakery with law offices upstairs. Tamale vendors, ice cream trucks. It's completely unique and incongruous. My favorite small business is Mercado's Discount Muffler and Flower shop on Alvarado. Insane. And it really feels like a neighborhood. It has its dangers, but I love it here.

Every Sunday my friend Lynne Littman and I meet at the farmers' market in Hollywood. We buy armloads of flowers and organic vegetables and torture ourselves by ending the morning petting the kittens and puppies they have for adoption on the corner. It's become a ritual that ends and begins the week in a semisane way. Lynne is a great friend. She's a wonderful filmmaker; she encourages and pushes me, listens to my complaints and ideas, and I do the same for her, I hope. We argue and we laugh a lot.

When I'm working, I spend way too much time on the freeway, driving from school to school. I teach ten to twelve classes per week, with ten kids per class, and spend a good deal of time thinking about the classes and how best to reach any given group or individual. I listen to music and language tapes. (I'm trying to learn to speak Irish Gaelic; it doesn't come naturally.)

When I'm not working, I try to get to the beach as often as possible, to walk or swim. I roller-skate sometimes. It's also where I get a lot of writing done. I go to the gym pretty regularly and have my writing group every Monday night. I have two cats that I adore, Abracadabra and Drum. We live in a little house with a small, unruly yard that I sometimes try to cultivate (at the moment I'm trying to grow tomatoes and strawberries) but mostly just watch the bushes and weeds take over the sidewalk. I try to see theater and performance, especially if friends are doing something, and to stay current with films, but I'm pretty happy to be home for the most part. I have a nine-year-old goddaughter and namesake, "Little Kate," and we try to spend as much time together as we can. She has her own room at my house, decorated with her artwork, full of books and toys. We're very close, and it's a relationship that has been a source of great joy in my life. My brothers and sister have started families of their own in the last few years, and the birth of their children has brought us back in contact after a period of estrangement. I'm very close to my nieces and nephews, though I don't get to see them as often as I'd like to. I love being Auntie Kate. I have an amazing community of friends, and even if we don't get to see each other often, it always feels current. I feel lucky every day to be in such community. I don't take it for granted. Somebody said, "My friends are my estate." That's precisely how I feel.

There is a place for romantic love, certainly; however, I rarely meet men older than eleven years old these days. I do have a few close male friends I keep in good contact with, and it's nice to have that infusion of male energy when I need it. My perfect relationship would be with someone who lives out of town and visits only one long weekend a month, with the occasional phone call. I had a relationship like that when I lived in New York, with a guy who lived in Maine. Perfect. I could never do the twenty-four-hours-a-day, seven-days-a-week thing. I'd go crazy. I like solitude too much. I'm pretty set in my ways.

Most of my women friends are older than I am, for some reason, and all my friends are role models in one way or another. I guess because I've always been surrounded by people who are older, I've never fit into one particular age group. I also have role models who are nine years old. I admire individuals and individual qualities.


One scenario of my fantasy of aging is a kind of Georgia O'Keeffe without the desert. I'd be on Inishmoor [one of the Aran Islands] in a thatched cottage, with cats and dogs and horses, looking out over the sea, writing and painting through the winters, reading everything, trudging down the hill to the pub on the rare occasion for hot whiskey and conversation. The summer would be filled with visitors—all the kids with their lovers and friends and sleeping bags—and travel, lots of travel.

The other scenario is as a National Geographic documentarian—that's actually my dream of a perfect life, young or old—shooting nature documentaries in the Serengeti, Nepal, Tibet—anywhere and everywhere. I would be completely happy sitting on a glacier or a mountaintop somewhere at dawn, staring through a 35mm lens at a polar bear or a temple or a mountain goat.

My perspective on aging is different from the fantasy, of course. It's that mixed bag of wisdom and loss, expansion and contraction. I think there is a tenderness that comes with age—not so much an abandonment of the fury, but a kind of tender eye toward the world, an awareness of its fragility, of each other's fragility—at least that's what I experience. Recently a friend of mine turned forty. He has AIDS, and we have lost quite a few friends and loved ones in the past decade. There was such a sweet sense of wonder and gratitude in that birthday—not spoken, really; it just quietly passed, but we felt it and acknowledged it.

There is also the awareness that the world may not, in fact, be your oyster. That you cannot do everything, be anything, and so must decide what space you can best occupy, what it is you do well, what it is you love, and what you want to concentrate on, having limited amounts of time and space. Life stops being casual and becomes a little more crafted and deliberate.

Another aspect of being a woman aging is that you become a little more invisible, and that is interesting—really interesting in terms of the kind of attention you are used to getting. It doesn't actually bother me, but I am aware of it and kind of fascinated. Not so easy to "girl" your way out of a speeding ticket, for example, and unaware, until it doesn't work, that it was a trick you used in the first place! Being a "pretty girl" parts waves for you in ways you don't quite fathom until they don't any more.

Traveling makes me feel alive. I long to be seized by landscape, by the raw energy that exists in the rock and bone and water of a place. I went to Greece a couple of years ago and felt addressed by the gods of each place—felt their capriciousness and power. I went to Ireland last year with my niece, and I have always had such a longing for the place that I expected to stand on the limestone or on the marble at Connemara and suddenly know everything. I expected to be addressed by the ancestors, to be shaken out of my idea of identity and be possessed by something truer, older, more authentic. I fell in love with the place, but the way one falls in love with the "other."

I went on a pilgrimage to the White Mountains once, to see the bristle-cone pine tree, because I'd heard it was the oldest living thing. I walked up the mountain through snow, convinced that if I managed, somehow, to be in relationship to that organism, I would learn more about myself than I ever could in a relationship with a man. Or a woman, for that matter. With any human. I've always known there are things in my nature I will never see reflected in other people, that I can't know in their company. I need a lot of solitude and the natural world. Working with the kids, too, I feel alive in another way. It makes me feel connected to the human race. Each kid I've worked with touches me in a very real way. I'm always moved at the ways in which they express themselves, by how brave they are, and by their resiliency. It isn't easy being a kid.

A kind of healing of my own past takes place, too, when I work with kids. It happens in small moments. I have the opportunity to be the person I needed at the age of eight or nine—the one to offer reassurance, love, encouragement. It's bearing witness. It's like the action in the present moment reaches back into the past moment of hurt or anguish, and a healing takes place. Because I didn't have a traditional upbringing—I wasn't really "brought up"; I had to figure most things out for myself—by the time I figured out what was in my control and what was not, I knew that it was up to me to find my tribe myself, the authentic family, my authentic life. The Bla Bla Club was really a godsend from 9 P.M. to 2 A.M. It was incredible music each night, and everyone was full of passion, belief, and amazing energy. It was a magic room that seemed to cut through boundaries of age, gender, color, class. It was open until 4 A.M., and at 2 A.M. people from all the bars would come in for breakfast, so it would fill with people from the various margins: the gay and lesbian bars, discos and jazz clubs, comedy clubs, and the street.

The upscale and trendy would eat their breakfast with the transgendered and homeless. We adopted each other. I was looked after in a lot of ways; I always had somewhere to go, someone to call if I needed to. When I was thirteen, a drag queen friend of mine taught me how to wear makeup, how to walk in heels. I was also, from the first, treated with respect—treated as a person with ideas, with dignity. I was exposed to different lifestyles, turned on to art and great music, was given a cultural education; most important, I was loved and welcomed.

At twenty-seven, I had a series of accidents and incidents: a car wreck, a near drowning, I almost chopped off my hand, I fell in love with the "wrong" man, my foot was operated on and I was immobilized for a time, my dog died, and finally I had a nervous breakdown, at which time I was diagnosed with depression. It was decided I was simply having a cumulative attack of my life. It was a very dark, almost unbearable time that I would not have survived without the help of my close friends. The blessing of that time was that I was forced to sit with myself, to really sit in the sorrow, the grief, the life, without distraction—no more drugs, alcohol, whatever—just sit with myself and figure out who was there, in the chemical soup. Clarity didn't come all at once, or all of a sudden. No big *Aha!* I'm still navigating those waters. Writing toward it, I hope.

My life hasn't really played out in the proper linear order; it's more like a snow globe, with all of these simultaneous separate events. When I turned thirty, it was the first birthday I ever paid any attention to. I decided I couldn't be thirty unless everything in my life was different. So I changed everything. Meaning for me, I began the process of taking my life seriously and figuring out what I wanted to say with it. I wrote my first performance piece (for other performers) that year and directed it. It was called *Without Gravity*. It was a small play, fragments really, about thresholds and dreams. I started toward my voice, finding my voice, feeling newly born, and at the age of thirty-three I went into menopause prematurely. That shook the globe a bit. Again finding myself at the end of so much, at a time when my life seemed to be beginning. No gradual transitions in my life. Lots of jump cuts, no dissolves.

What I want to say to other women who have passions and want to pursue them is that there will always be people who, for a variety of reasons, will want to talk you out of them. Friends, family, who will be devil-in-your-ear deceptive because they "have your best interest at heart," who are afraid you will be hurt, who want to keep you near them, or safe—whatever. Life hurts. To thine own self be true. You will pay a price, certainly, for every pursuit of every passion, but if you don't follow your passion to wherever it leads you, you will pay for it in different ways. The only regrets I have are the times I said no—when I should have said yes—out of fear, out of a sense of propriety, of responsibility. Out of fear, plain and simple. Don't compromise. Follow the golden ball into the forest, as a wise person once told me.

Children are very important to me. When I was little, I imagined that when I grew up, I'd have six or seven kids. I have always taught kids. I've helped raise several kids from the time I was thirteen. I remember once telling a friend that I had a feeling I would not have children, and she said to me, "Then you better be brilliant." I felt it like a knife in the heart—this belief she had that a woman had to produce something extraordinary in order to be seen as having value in the world.

I always wanted to give birth to a child and took for granted that I would one day. Then menopause hit with great force totally out of the blue, and I was devastated. I went to a fertility doctor at one point, thinking maybe I might go that route, and as I sat in the waiting room watching women come out in tears, with these anguished expressions, like they had failed and were ashamed, I knew that it wasn't my road. I had to figure out why this, of all things, was my lot. I figure there is a reason. A lesson. Not to say I believe in a divine plan, but if I look at the theme and shape of my life, it's ironic.

I think part of the lesson is that I don't have to be the mother to really love a kid. I have no problem whatsoever falling madly in love with other people's children. I may adopt a loose child or two one day if I am ever financially secure. Who knows? But for now it seems that I am meant to be teaching my 110 kids a week. I don't feel that my worth is determined by whether I fulfill my biological destiny, any more than I feel my worth is determined by being or not being with a man. I have never felt that way, but the end of the choice was a loss I experienced as a death.

I guess my definition of success would be not having to go look for funding. Not having to figure out what to sell to pay the rent. Not having to live paycheck to paycheck. That's a part of it. The burden of poverty lifting. And the ability and opportunity to do what you love. The ability and opportunity to be of service. That's one that I've struggled with. In the eighties when all the wretched psychological jargon infected the national lexicon, if one's instinct was to be of service to others, it meant that you were either a religious fanatic, in which case it was assumed you had at some point sustained some serious damage, or you were "codependent." I have really struggled with other people's models and definitions of success. I'm still struggling. Living in Hollywood doesn't help. It's so disproportionate to any real standard. I am forever being possessed by the voices that say I should be further along in a CA-REER. I need a new car!! I should be able to buy a house!!! I'm too old to be doing what I'm doing!!!! I try to filter them out; protect myself from toxic industry fallout. An accurate way for me to measure success is by looking to the Three Pure Precepts in Buddhism: Do not commit evil. Do good. Do good for others. If I can say at the end of every day I have fulfilled that directive, then I am successful. Creative expression means everything to me. I don't know how else to say it. When I can't write or speak, I make collages of images. If I'm struggling with something I can't find words for, I can usually find a way to express it visually. Sometimes they come together: words and images, color, light. It's compulsory; it isn't a choice. It's my only language—the only way I know how to function, how to be in the world, make sense of the world.

In the next decade I look forward to seeing how all the kids in my life grow, who they become, the choices they make. I look forward to those relationships deepening—to all my relationships and friendships aging and deepening. I look forward to the work ahead. I feel that I haven't hit my stride yet. I want to get in there and really do my best. I feel that the best of my life is yet to come. I look forward to whatever is in store. I really do. Good, bad: bring it on.

# The Author

*Cathleen Rountree* is a writer, visual artist and photographer, cultural mythologist and film scholar, lecturer and educator, and consultant to both aspiring and established writers. She is the author of seven books, including the highly acclaimed decade series on women and aging: *On Women Turning 40: Coming into Our Fullness; On Women Turning 50: Celebrating Midlife Discoveries; On Women Turning 60: Embracing the Age of Fulfillment;* and *On Women Turning 70: Honoring the Voices of Wisdom.* She is currently writing a book about the confluence and interrelationship between film and psychology. She lives in Northern California and may be contacted through her website: http://home.earthlink.net/~crountree.